Pelican Books

UNDERSTANDING VOLUNTARY ORGANIZATIONS

Charles Handy is Visiting Professor at the London Business School, a writer and broadcaster and a consultant to a wide variety of organizations in business, government and the voluntary sector.

Born in Dublin, he was educated at Oxford and the Massachusetts Institute of Technology (Sloan School of Management). He has worked for Shell International and as an economist for the Anglo-American Corporation. In 1967 he joined the London Business School to start and direct the Sloan Programme there and to teach managerial psychology and development. He was appointed Professor in 1972 and Governor in 1974. He is the author of *Understanding Organizations* (Penguin, 1976), *Gods of Management* (1979), *Taking Stock* (1983), *The Future of Work* (1984) and, with Robert Aitken, *Understanding Schools as Organizations* (Penguin, 1986). He was Chairman of the Advisory Panel of the Management Development Unit of the National Council for Voluntary Organizations until 1986 and has worked with and advised many voluntary organizations.

Charles Handy lives in London and Norfolk with his wife Elizabeth. They have two children.

CHARLES HANDY

UNDERSTANDING
VOLUNTARY
ORGANIZATIONS

Penguin Books

PENGUIN BOOKS
Published by the Penguin Group
27 Wrights Lane, London w8 5TZ, England
Viking Penguin Inc., 40 West 23rd Street, New York, New York 10010, USA
Penguin Books Australia Ltd, Ringwood, Victoria, Australia
Penguin Books Canada Ltd, 2801 John Street, Markham, Ontario, Canada L3R 1B4
Penguin Books (NZ) Ltd, 182–190 Wairau Road, Auckland 10, New Zealand

Penguin Books Ltd, Registered Offices: Harmondsworth, Middlesex, England

First published 1988

Typeset in Linotron Times

Typeset, printed and bound in Great Britain by
Hazell Watson & Viney Limited
Member of BPCC plc
Aylesbury, Bucks, England

Contents

Foreword

In 1977, shortly after I became Director-General of the National Council for Voluntary Organizations, I began to look for someone who had the talent and reputation to recommend how NCVO might assist its membership of local and national organizations to improve the management of their affairs. This was no easy task, since for years (perhaps for ever) many voluntary bodies had considered themselves to be quite different from other organizations. One aspect of this difference was the reluctance to recognize the need for any advice or assistance with the development or management of the organization.

Today voluntary organizations are relatively fashionable, by which I mean that since the end of the Second World War the fortunes of voluntary organizations have fluctuated. A fully fledged cradle-to-grave Welfare State would have found little room for voluntary organizations. At the other end of the spectrum a privatized welfare system would change the nature of voluntary bodies, driving them to become ever more competitive bidders for contracts to care for the elderly, children, the countryside or the inner city. Voluntary organizations have been subject to many of the same pulls and pushes that have affected industry and other sectors of society over the past forty years.

Charles Handy was one of the first people to understand this, to see what lessons might be learned from management in industry and commerce and to see what is different about the voluntary sector. I am indebted to Foster Murphy, now Director of the Volunteer Centre, then a deputy director of NCVO, for introducing me to Charles Handy and recommending that he should lead a working party to see how best voluntary organizations' management needs might be met.

There followed the Handy Working Party Report and the establishment of the NCVO Management Development Unit led by Patrick Wright. If imitation flatters, then Charles Handy should be flattered, since advice centres and units for the benefit of the management of voluntary organizations have mushroomed. Some I would not touch with a bargepole, but the point has been well and truly made. Voluntary organizations need management, and their managers can benefit from help and advice.

Ten years later the book *Understanding Voluntary Organizations* demonstrates that Charles Handy has stuck with it. This book has the benefit of a decade of unrivalled experience of working with the voluntary sector. In addition Charles Handy suggests ways in which voluntary bodies might organize themselves that will influence others as patterns of work in our changing society.

Since becoming Director-General of the Save the Children Fund I have sought and valued Charles Handy's advice and that of the NCVO Management Development Unit he inspired. *Understanding Voluntary Organizations* is an excellent addition to the range of assistance and support available to those of us involved with these interesting and unusual creatures called voluntary organizations.

Nicholas Hinton
Director-General
The Save the Children Fund

January 1988

Acknowledgements

I shall always be indebted to the many voluntary organizations and their leaders who helped me to understand them better and so to write this book. In particular I am grateful to Nicholas Hinton and Foster Murphy, who introduced me to the world of voluntary organizations during their time at the National Council for Voluntary Organizations, and to Patrick Wright, who directed the Management Development Unit and who helped so much to make sense of that world for me.

In the end, however, all books like this one are an anthology, with some interpretation, of other people's work, of other writers and teachers in this area. I have cited the most important ones, for me, in the text but there are always others who have eaten their way into my subconscious and been forgotten, including the students who by their arguments have improved my ideas, and the clients who have turned my consultancy into a learning opportunity for me. To all these anonymous ones I owe my thanks.

Especially am I grateful to Elizabeth, who helped in so many ways to bring this book to reality and who, as my wife, had to live with my endless fascination for the voluntary world, and to Andrew Franklin, both my sternest critic and the most patient and supportive of editors.

Charles Handy
Diss, Norfolk
April 1988

1

It is Good to be Different

'Organizations are boring.' 'Management is only manipulation under another name.' 'The voluntary world can well do without both.' They don't always put it so explicitly, but you don't have to be long in voluntary work to hear such voices speaking. The sentiment is clear and understandable; the logic is not.

Organizations there have to be. One man, one woman, on their own, can do so little. And it were better that things were organized than disorganized, for that helps nobody; which means management, to neglect which is to bring unnecessary pain on oneself and others.

This is where the sentiment comes in. Do organizations have to be grey bureaucracies? Does management have to mean the dictatorship of the functionaries or control by the balance sheet? The answer must be no, if there is to be any hope for the human spirit. Maybe, in its desire to reject the stereotypes of 'organization' and 'management', the voluntary world has a clue to a better order.

Can we take what we know about people and organizations and put it together in a better way? Can we talk about getting things done effectively without even using the words 'manager' and 'management', with all their loaded overtones? Is there lurking in the voluntary world a better theory of organizing? If so, then this book is one clue to its ingredients, for it seeks to unravel the underlying causes of things organizational and to show how a better understanding can lead to better practice.

This first chapter is designed to provide a taste of the book as a whole, a rationale for its existence and a guide to its contents, all in a few pages, under these headings:

- Who needs management?
- The perils of voluntarism.
- The confusion of categories.
- There has to be a better way.
- The shape of the book.

Who needs management?

'A voluntary organization – that's a contradiction in itself!'

That is to carry cynicism too far. Were voluntary organizations as chaotic, anarchic and inefficient as their more cynical detractors like to think they are, we wouldn't be spending so much time or money on them – see Box 1.1. Even the British are not as masochistic as that.

There is, however, a taste of truth concealed in the cynicism. Voluntary organizations do like to emphasize the 'voluntary' and play down the 'organization', believing that the ends are more important than the means, that the cause is what matters and, if it matters enough, that it will justify any lack of organization and may even, like a purifying emetic, get rid of it.

It goes deeper than that in some places. To many in the voluntary sector, organization means management, and management reeks of authoritarianism, of capitalism, of business and bureaucracy. The feelings don't even have to be that political. 'Management' to many sounds very like manipulation. Who amongst us likes to be 'managed'? It sounds all too reminiscent of those mule-trains for which, it is reputed, the first management manuals were written.

The essence of a voluntary organization, after all, is that people are there because they want to be there. Many of them are paid, perhaps as many as 250,000 full-time in total, but most of those are professionals of one sort or another who could probably earn more in other organizations, and have chosen their place deliberately. If you join something because you believe in its cause and its values, because you want to, you are not about to submit yourself to some anonymous authority, to subject yourself to bureaucratic whims or to do, automatically, what someone else tells you to do. A voluntary organization, one instinctively feels, should be a citizen organization where everyone is fundamentally equal, whatever their formal role.

Indeed, in a committed organization, some feel, management should be unnecessary. A family who love each other care for each other and need the very minimum of management or organization. It all just happens – or should do. Even if management is necessary, the argument goes on, it hardly needs people called managers; for what is management but common sense, an ability which anyone of any

---

Box 1.1 How many voluntary organizations are there?

Surprisingly, perhaps, nobody knows! There are 150,000 registered charities in Britain with an annual income of over £9 billion but they are but the registered tip of the iceberg.

The Times (7 May 1985) considers that there are 350,000 voluntary organizations of all types, including local self-help and campaigning groups.

The Volunteer Centre's research sample in 1981 suggested that 1 in 5 adults do something with voluntary groups each week and that over half get involved in some way during the year.

Government grants to the voluntary sector run at over £1,000 million a year.

There are half a million people involved as volunteers with youth work alone.

However you count it, it's big stuff!

---

maturity can conjure up when the need arises? Management, after all, they might say, is like making love – it's something we all find we can do when we need to, even if some choose to make a speciality out of it.

These feelings are understandable although perhaps too reminiscent of that strange and uniquely British admiration for the amateur and their snobbish disdain for the professional, for industry and therefore, especially, for the professional industrial manager. It is noteworthy that none of the old-established British institutions like the professions, the universities and schools, the Civil Service or the armed services use the word 'manager' to denote any but the humblest of roles such as store manager or office manager. The top people are given curious titles like dean or principal, vice-chancellor, under-secretary or partner, which all in the know realize to be titles to conjure with but don't carry any of the nasty overtones of manager.

Voluntary organizations, however, would be foolish to throw the baby out with the managerial bath-water. While renouncing many of the assumptions which underlie the management of businesses they should not ignore the fact that they themselves are organizations made up of people and that there are things known about the way people interact with each other or with organizations which are likely to hold true in their world as well as in that of business. It may not feel good to be managed but it is still better to be organized than disorganized.

Similarly, voluntary organizations are not businesses, but they do have clients, they provide services and they have to finance themselves in one way or another. It makes just as much sense to ask a voluntary organization what its strategy is as it does to ask a business. It is not sinful to be businesslike.

Most of those who work in these organizations are not so naïve, although at the radical end of the spectrum there is a powerful ideology which wants to reject anything which smacks of inequality, be it different rates of pay, earmarked jobs, decision-making powers or even the right to do what you are best at doing. This leads to the kind of agonizing dilemma of the church choir which hesitates to say 'no' to the volunteer soloist even though her voice is barely adequate and there is a much better, but more modest, soprano available.

The perils of this tyranny of democracy are well described in *What a Way to Run a Railroad*, a book which is subtitled 'An Analysis of Radical Failure' but also provides some clues to a better way. The story in Box 1.2 is one of the examples given in this stimulating little book.

Box 1.2 Egalitarianism gone crazy

Another pitfall we've come across is the argument that, because bourgeois theatre is skilful, the development of skills is bourgeois. It is even sometimes argued that a lack of skill is good because it demystifies the theatrical process. When we first started, there was this low level of skill in the group . . . for quite a long time we rationalized this stage of development (which most groups go through) into a historical dogma. Eventually, we realized that the belief that if your ideas are correct then it 'doesn't matter how well or badly you put them over' is false.

From Richard Seyd, 'The Theatre of Red Ladder', quoted in Charles Landry *et al.*, *What a Way to Run a Railroad* (Comedia, 1985).

It is sad, but in the well-meant name of democracy much harm can be done to efficiency and effectiveness. For instance, it is easy in the name of democracy to confuse consent and consensus. Effective democracy relies on consent. He or she who governs does so with the trust and consent of those who are governed, who have the right and power to get rid of the governor when that trust and respect are exhausted. Those in charge take the decisions, which can be implemented only with the consent of those who carry them out. 'You cannot tell me what to do,' said a colleague, 'only ask me, and I can refuse.' It is difficult but it works very well with the right person in charge.

Consensus, on the other hand, requires that everyone takes every decision. It is a travesty of democracy, time-consuming, irritating and fraught with politics and factions. It is usually so frustrating that it is quickly allowed to degenerate into an autocracy or the dictatorship of a clique if only to allow something, anything, to happen. Democracy is a dangerous slogan on its own.

The perils of voluntarism

Reject management and all its ways and you invite not only the tyranny of democracy but two other perils of voluntarism: strategic delinquency and the servant syndrome, both of which can end up by abusing individuals and organizations.

Strategic delinquency

It is too easy, without proper thought and proper decision-making processes, to put the ethos of the place in front of the goals to be achieved. 'The cause is all,' it is said; 'to stand for something is perhaps more important than to achieve'; 'to be in there striving is what counts'. This sounds noble and often is but it allows one comfortably to ignore any definition of success, comfortably because any definition of success implies the possibility of failure. There can, however, be a lot of pain wrapped up in that comfort, because without any definition of success how can anyone ever look back on a week or a year and say 'that was well done'? How can anyone rest content, ever? How can there be any end to striving? To bring peace to the world is the sort of task that only gods should take on; lesser mortals would be wise to set less ambitious goals lest they feel forever frustrated.

Is it because of this lack of any possibility of success that voluntary organizations are so often not the fun-filled places of enthusiasm you might think they should be, but the abodes of careworn caring people pushing some stone forever uphill?

Worse, strategic delinquency can lead to strategic seduction. Anyone who offers money for the cause is welcome, and more money is even more welcome. Many voluntary organizations have found themselves becoming the agents of their paymasters, be those paymasters a government department, a local authority or the Manpower Services Commission. Having no clear goals or precise definitions of the task to be done leaves the door open to what amounts to a take-over. What price democracy and voluntarism when he who pays the piper is free to call the tune?

Box 1.3 Disabling organizations?

Ivan Illich described how professionals need clients in order to survive and cynically suggested that they create and define problems, diseases and deficiencies which they, and they only, have the skills to put right. They disable their clients in order to enable them, creating thereby a spurious dependency and problems which need never have been invented.

Voluntary organizations can be lured into this trap by strategic delinquency. Sure of themselves and of what they have to offer, they need opportunities to help and people to be helped. Do they ever discover unnecessary evils or keep people needing them longer than they should? Without clear aims and measures of success, it is hard to tell.

The servant syndrome

The voluntary world is in the gift economy. People give of their time and their skills for no money or for very little money. In such a world, poverty becomes almost a badge of virtue; we must make do and mend rather than invest in better equipment, better premises, better people. More careful thought might suggest that more investment could lead to better delivery, but without proper managerial-type disciplines this calculation can never be made. The result? A sort of built-in inefficiency as part of the culture and an ethos which says that everyone should do their own housekeeping, their own stamp-licking and typing – which, when you think of it, is probably an abuse of their real talents.

The other feature of the servant syndrome is the constant need to respond. You are there to give and to serve, goes the feeling, and there are so many who need what you have to offer. It is a bottomless pit, down which many fall. The loneliness of caring is well documented, as are the cases of 'burn-out' and the depression that comes from a never-ending task. It does no good to self or to others to be always working at the end of one's energies; but how can it be OK to say 'no' when there are no boundaries to the task? Weeks of 168 hours are not feasible for anyone, but the guilt of unfinished business is cruel.

We all need stability zones for recreation, but without boundaries there is no end. It is one of the key tasks of management to set boundaries, to define what has to be done, what can be done and what does not need to be done. Without that sort of discipline we abuse ourselves and those we try to help.

Ideological fanaticism

To these two perils one can sometimes add a third: ideological fanaticism. At times the rejection of management and all it stands for goes to extremes. Those who came of age in 1968 and moved into the world of alternative organizations in the 1970s developed a new set of bad words:*

● 'Success': to be successful was to risk contamination and to compromise your principles. It was better to stay pure and fail; indeed, perhaps the only way to stay pure is to fail, to be a 'drabbie' rather than a 'yuppie'. Thus

---

* I am indebted to one of that generation, David Harker, for pointing this out to me.

it was that many preferred to tilt against the windmills of society instead of building ones that worked better.

- 'Structures': structures imply hierarchy, they suggest that one individual is entitled to more authority than another. Ironically, the lack of structures allowed informal power élites to arise, cabals to be created, deals to be fixed in private and organizations to become corrupted.
- 'Professionalism': professions got a bad name in the 1970s, for creating dependence and for assuming incapacity in others. To believe should be enough, and so the voluntary world became the refuge of Britain's favoured species, the enthusiastic amateurs, whereas professionalism proper means doing things well.
- 'Leadership': community was all, togetherness was what mattered; no one person should try to impose his or her views. Indeed, leadership is risky; it means exposing oneself to rejection and to unpopularity. Leaderless groups, however, can become endless encounter groups more interested in discussing why than in doing it, which was the experience of many in the 1970s.

Link ideological fanaticism of this kind to strategic delinquency and the servant syndrome and you end up with the frustrated, embittered, exhausted and ineffective idealists who at one time epitomized so much of the voluntary world. It need not be like that. Virtue does not have to be so painful, *if* it is sensibly organized.

The confusion of categories

We add confusion to the pain if we unconsciously think that there is one thing called a voluntary organization and try to think up rules for running it. A moment's reflection makes it clear that it would be absurd to pretend that all voluntary organizations are alike. There is little logic in grouping together the Royal National Institute for the Blind and the small co-operative trying to start a radical newspaper in the living-room.

There is in fact a sense in which the voluntary sector is defined negatively – by what it is not, rather than by what it is. It is not profit-seeking, it is not government-run, it is

---

Box 1.4 What are voluntary organizations?

Voluntary organizations fall into five categories – with a lot of overlap.

There are the service providers, be they the Spastics Society, Dr Barnardo's, the National Trust or the Lifeboat Institution. Some of those will have over 1,000 paid staff and depend as much on government grants as on voluntary contributions for their existence.

There are those concerned with research and advocacy, ranging from the Child Poverty Action Group to the Campaign for Nuclear Disarmament to radical action groups in local communities or specialist journals.

Then there are the self-help groups that give support and assistance, to single parents, for example, or to those caring for sufferers from disease, or the groups which have sprung up to support the unemployed.

There is also another form of self-help group, that of those who share a common interest or enthusiasm, be it for playing cricket, gardening or kite-flying. The clubs and societies for leisure interests don't think of themselves as voluntary organizations or as volunteers but they are there from choice not for pay and there are lots of them, an important part of our society – see Box 1.5.

Lastly there are the intermediary bodies, like the councils for voluntary service, which are there to provide help with skills and advice on policy.

Many will fall into more than one category. Shelter, for example, is both a campaigning organization for better housing and a provider of accommodation and advice to the homeless.

No wonder the scene is confusing to the outsider when such a wide variety consorts under the same umbrella name.

---

not owned by anyone. That leaves a multitude of possibilities, maybe 350,000 of them, of widely different types – see Box 1.4.

Volunteers play different roles in the different types of organization. In some they are the core professionals (as in marriage guidance or the Samaritans). In some they *are* the organization, being both the clients and the providers (as in Alcoholics Anonymous, Gingerbread and other mutual-support organizations). In others they hold the account-ability of the organization by sitting on its management committee, leaving paid professionals to do the day-to-day work (as in Dr Barnardo's and the big service-providing charities). In yet others they are the supporters and fund-raisers rather than the core staff (as in Christian Aid and Oxfam).

It does not make any sense at all to try to formulate an all-embracing theory in practice for all voluntary organizations. That is why this book offers only a skeleton. Not only is it OK to be different from the organizations of business and government, it is OK to be different from other voluntary bodies. In fact, every organization is different, just as every human being is a different personality even though the bone structure is the same for all. Organizations have to develop their own personality if they are going to mean anything to their members. There is no such thing as a universal manual for organizations, and God forbid that there should ever be one.

Nevertheless, there are things in common, both at the level of the skeleton and at other levels too. It would be silly to pretend that in spite of their very proper individual differences you could not group organizations together for some purposes, just as it makes sense in some contexts to talk about women as opposed to men, or those who are musical and less musical, as long as it is remembered that the distinctions are important for only some contexts and not for all.

Box 1.4 provides a conventional categorization of vol-untary organizations. Here is another one, with more relevance to organization theory. There are three broad types of voluntary activity:

- *Mutual support* – those organizations which are created in order to put people with a particular problem or enthusiasm in touch with others like themselves who can give them understanding, advice, support and encouragement. Many voluntary organizations start this way, be they for sufferers from multiple sclerosis, parents of drug addicts, or alcoholics. The associations to do with hobbies and sports also fall into this category; model railway enthusiasts, Bugatti car owners and kite-flyers have their support networks too – indeed, the network is what it is all about.
- *Service delivery* – the biggest and most visible of the voluntary organizations are in the business of providing services to those in need: the RNIB, Mountain Rescue, the Royal National Lifeboat Institution, Save the Children, the Marriage Guidance Council, the Spastics Society and many more. Some of these organizations have so many paid staff (the Spastics Society has over 1,200) that it is hard at first to tell them apart from their counterparts in the statutory sector.
- *Campaigning* – some organizations, of which CND is the best-known example, were created to campaign for a cause or to act as a pressure group in a particular interest, be it against racism in education or in favour of women's rights.

The categorization is crude, of course, and many voluntary organizations fit all three categories or slip unwittingly into a fourth. Is CND, for instance, only about campaigning or is it also a mutual-aid organization, a support network for enthusiasts for peace? There lies the rub, for in this unconscious blending of the categories lies much organizational confusion.

The fact is that each of the categories carries with it an unspoken and implicit assumption about the nature of organizations and how they ought to run.

A mutual-support group needs only the minimum amount of organization to service the members, to find reasons for meetings, to send out occasional circulars, to let its existence be known to people who might need it. The

---

Box 1.5 Mutual support in leisure

In their fascinating study of leisure interest groups, Jeff Bishop and Paul Hoggett found that in Kingswood, Surrey, with a population of around 85,000 there were 300 leisure interest groups involving perhaps 28,500 people. Only 37 per cent involved sporting activities. There were, for example, five photography societies, eight drama societies, four chess clubs and five gardening clubs.

In north-east Leicester, with a different type of population, they located 228 groups in a total population of approximately 68,000. At one centre there were three football clubs, one largely Asian cricket club, a gardening club, a lapidary society, an Irish society, a community orchestra, a photography club, an audio-visual club, a junior gym club and two yoga clubs.

The authors list 112 activities ranging from morris dancing through lace-making to computer games around which local clubs, societies and associations have been formed. They claim, with much justification, that this is a neglected but important part of British life. Organizations which exist primarily for their members, and consume their own products, are as much to do with just being there as with doing anything.

J. Bishop and P. Hoggett, *Organizing around Enthusiasms: Mutual Aid in Leisure* (Comedia, 1986).

---

only qualification for membership is that you fit the description of the organization. Any single parent can join an association for single parents; any alcoholic can join Alcoholics Anonymous. No one is going to vet them for intelligence, analyse their job record or give them an aptitude test.

Mutual-aid groups do not want to be 'managed'; they detest the thought and are reluctant to divert any of their caring energies to the tasks of administration or of organization, which seem to them to be a distraction. At most they want to be 'serviced' by a secretary or a co-ordinator, with everyone joining in for any policy discussions that might be required.

Service-delivery organizations, on the other hand, are all about organization. They exist to meet a need, to provide help to those who need it. They take pride in being professional, effective and low-cost. It follows that they need to be selective about their recruits, demanding in their review of standards, prepared to reprimand where necessary, even to dismiss someone whose work is inadequate.

You cannot join the delivery part of these organizations just because you agree with their work. They want and need professional qualifications and will pay proper, or nearly proper, salaries for them. You can help, by all means. You can raise money, mail literature, badger local authorities, be elected to their council; but you cannot, by your choice, join the core.

These are 'managed' organizations – they have to be. They will therefore have within them much of the paraphernalia of bureaucracy: jobs which carry formal definitions, with formal responsibilities and formal accountability to other bodies; the impersonal feel of an organization which can continue to operate in the same way even if the individuals in it change and move.

Campaigning organizations are led rather than managed. True, they need their administration to be done effectively, meetings well organized, literature well written and printed on time, but these are subordinate functions. The essence of the organization is that of adherents to a cause, focused on a leader, often a charismatic one whose personality infects the organization. The only qualification for belonging is that you believe, and the more believers the better. It is, in fact, more a movement than an organization; or, at least, the organization is but the formal part which serves the movement, efficiently but preferably invisibly. Organization is, as with mutual-aid organizations, a necessary chore, to be done but not too obviously.

Box 1.6 The group meeting

The local single parents' group was in distress. The room which had been theirs for meetings, events and parties and had acted as their informal centre had been reclaimed by the landlord for his own use.

An informal meeting of some of the core group was arranged one evening in the home of one of the parents. As was the custom, all the children of the parents came too. They were, after all, the 'badges of belonging'; you could hardly be a single parent in need if you weren't obviously surrounded by your children. But it did make the meeting rather chaotic, since no one was prepared to be crèche minder for the evening – everyone wanted to be in on the discussion.

Ideas abounded for new ways of finding facilities. But who was to do the follow-up work after the meeting? Who was, as it were, the executive officer of the group? There were no volunteers. As single parents they were far too busy scraping together a living, looking after their children and tending the home to have time to do another job of sorts. Should they find someone, then, who wasn't a single parent to work for them? That would be to breach the most basic rule of their group: only single parents could be involved. Even ex-single parents were excluded.

The meeting took only one decision in the end: to meet next month at the home of one of the other members. So, one felt, it would go on, for no one wanted what was to them the 'chore' of organizing, and maybe meeting together was what it was all about anyway.

Each set of assumptions hangs together. And, as this book will make clear, there are different ways of organizing different structures and cultures for each set. The confusion and the problems start when the sets overlap.

That happens all too frequently because organizations do

not usually stand still or stick to their last. They tend to grow and develop as they prosper. Members of a mutual-aid organization, for instance, will begin to think that in addition to supporting one another in distress they ought to do something practical about it, start a school, create a hospital, build a home. Some of the members will then want to do something about the lack of public appreciation of their predicament, may even want to get some laws changed or taxes eased. Quite sensibly and naturally the mutual-aid society has moved into service delivery and into campaigning. The logic is clear, but the clash of assumptions can be heard from miles away – see Box 1.7.

It can work the other way. A campaigning organization finds it cannot rest content with words. It must put its actions where its mouth is and move into an appropriate service delivery, or at least offer a support network to those who suffer. Des Wilson has said that a campaigning organization has a moral responsibility to put its expertise into practice, to inject it into the system and pass it on to the public.

'What I loved about Shelter', he said, 'was that combination of daily helping families and campaigning. It was a wonderful healthy balance.'

You can see his point, but the moral combination works only if there are in effect two separate organizations doing the two separate tasks under one umbrella. To the director on top of the umbrella, and to the world outside, it is one organization, but to the wise director it is two organizations underneath.

When voluntary organizations talk about the importance of values they are right. But values become the subject of an argument whenever the categories get combined and confused. A pure mutual-aid organization has no problems about values until it starts to try to provide a service. The assumptions and values conflict, because it becomes necessary to define what is meant by success, which you cannot do unless you are clear what it is you are trying to do and at what cost and to what standards.

'If we save one child from dying in the gutter, this society is justified,' cried a member at the AGM.

'What – even if it involved neglecting a hundred children not yet in the gutter?' replied the chairperson. It was a concealed debate between a campaign and a service-delivery outlook.

Box 1.7 The threefold organization

Over a century ago it had started – an association for the young and the lonely of our cities, provided only that they were female and Christian. What they needed were places to forgather to find fellowship, friendship and Christian ways. It had moved on since then, running projects for women as well as a string of cheap but decent hostels for women of any faith. It was involved in campaigning internationally for the cause of women generally, for peace and for better international relations.

As a result some of the meetings were interesting. Proposals for tighter budgeting, more realistic financing of building projects and better evaluation of standards of hostels, occupancy rates and returns on capital alternated, not always harmoniously, with pleas for the local members to be more involved, for space to be allocated for prayer meetings and social clubs at no charge. Should non-members be allowed to stay? Should non-Christians be allowed?

What was the point of an association which let in everyone? some asked. What was the point of hostels half-empty? came back the rejoinder. Well, then, what about all this advocacy – so loud, so radical, so expensive? What had it to do with fellowship – wasn't it only a glamorous distraction from their real business, international junketing in place of caring?

The passion in their voices drowned out the logic. Personalities became more important than argument, as often happens when organizations use one mechanism for three very different tasks.

Organizations can, of course, keep it simple and therefore straightforward. Some of the most successful do just that.

Alcoholics Anonymous sticks to what it does so well. It is not trying to become a campaigning organization, although the temptation must at times be great. The Samaritans do only what they do so well. They have not moved into the hospice movement, although there could be a logic in such a move.

Most organizations, however, have grown like Topsy and end up as some sort of amalgam of all three categories. There is nothing wrong with that. It may indeed, as Des Wilson says, be the only way to stay honest. It will, however, make life more complicated because the organizational assumptions will clash.

This book will suggest that federalism is one way forward, a way of functioning that allows differences to work in common harness. Federalism, unfortunately, is not too familiar a concept to the British, who have always seen it as a device for keeping your enemies separated and weak, even though history has always proved them wrong.

Federalism is interestingly different from monarchy. Federalism sees differences as a strength, provided they are differences about the how and not the what, the means and not the ends. Monarchy would prefer a replica organization with similar rules for all. That is because in monarchical situations power and responsibility are delegated from the centre to the parts. In federalism it is the other way round; the centre gets the bits which other parts cannot do. Federal organizations are tight–loose structures, keeping a very few things tight and allowing the maximum of autonomy, believing that it is a vision not rules which binds people together. Monarchical and bureaucratic systems put more faith in the rules. Monarchical ideas build factories. Federalism prefers teams operating under a common flag.

These differences will be explored in more detail later on. They are important because it is the high irony of the voluntary world that it has chosen to use the monarchical/bureaucratic model of organization even though all its instincts repudiate it. Perhaps this is because it knows no other.

There has to be a better way

Organizations are not obvious. They cannot be taken for granted. That is one message of this book. The second is that we each of us carry around an implicit, unspoken idea of what organizing involves and of what an organization is. This idea comes from our early experience, perhaps, or from a stereotype of how things work in the rest of the world, which may in turn come from hearsay or from films or from newspapers. The idea, however, may be wrong, or at least wrong for where we are at the moment. We need to bring these assumptions out into the open and compare them with alternatives. Organizations don't all have to be run like factories.

It would, however, be folly to think that much useful work can be done without an organization. Goodwill is not enough, democratic ideas are not enough, hard work is not enough. Without the right organization, great ideals breed only great frustration – see Box 1.8.

Box 1.8 A volunteer's lament

I am a committed, sincere and honest person. I deeply believe in what we are doing. So do all the others, I am quite sure. We work here, many of us for nothing, others for not much more, because the task is so important, so urgent.

Why then is it so frustrating? Why do I come away feeling angry, bruised, ineffectual? Why do we seem to spend so much of our time talking, or doing menial jobs like putting papers into envelopes, or arguing about trivia, even bitching about each other and complaining about the way things are done or not done?

How can such good people create such bad work?

Any wholesale rejection of the ideas of management must be naïve. None the less the instinctual desire to put management in its place and to make it subservient to the cause and to the people involved has to be right. It may go further than that; it may be a gut feeling that the whole language and philosophy of management are wrong, not only for voluntary organizations but for all organizations. Maybe it is time for a new look at the way we talk about all organizations, and therefore think about them, a new look pioneered by the organizations of the voluntary sector.

The language of management is, when you think about it, odd. It is unnatural, to begin with. Only the English have the word 'manage' as part of their language and even they, when they use it colloquially, do not mean any of the things set out in the management textbooks: 'How did you manage today?' 'Did you manage to get the car fixed?' means 'Did you find a way to . . .?' 'Managing the house' means 'looking after the house'. Nothing about motivating, inspiring, structuring, controlling, setting standards or participative decision-making.

Look deeper into those textbooks and manuals. The implicit model of the organization is an engineering one. The organization is conceived of as a sophisticated clock or engine, with interlocking parts, something which can, in theory, be designed to be perfect (were it not for the unpredictability of some of those human parts). The organization can be 'designed'. People are 'human resources'. There are 'plans' and 'control systems', 'outputs' and 'inputs', and organization charts which look quite similar to the layout diagrams you will see in power-stations or process plants. The language of organization theory has, in the past, been that of engineering and more recently of electrical engineering (with its talk of feedback loops, pulses and currents).

Language is important. It is the outward and visible sign of an inward way of thinking. 'Management' is part of that language and therefore symbolic of that way of thinking. It implies that control of people is similar to the control of things, that people are resources to be counted, deployed and utilized.

No wonder that it sticks in the gullet if you are one of those meant to be managed. No wonder our older institutions shun it. No wonder other countries keep it as a foreign word – *le management*. It should be no surprise, when you think about it, that the organizations which use it most, in industry, are seldom counted among the best of British, that those activities for which the British are notable – the arts, journalism, pop music, photography and fashion, financial services and consultancy, the professions and education – are the most sparing in their use of the word and in their use of the concepts.

Things are changing, however. The new words in the organizational literature are words like 'culture', 'shared values', 'networks and alliances', 'power and influence', 'federalism', 'compromise and consent' and, most crucially, 'leadership' rather than 'management'. These are not the metaphors of engineering but those of political theory, and they symbolize a new way of thinking about organizations – as societies or communities rather than as machines or warehouses. New words are the heralds of change, and these words point to a revolution in the way we think about organizations.

The revolution has not yet happened. So far the new language has been but a gloss on the old, a kind of grease for the machine. Nevertheless it is interesting that the books which are starting to use this language are the new best-sellers, have indeed been the first books about organizations ever to be in the top-ten list. It is as if managers have sensed that the theorists are at last writing about the world as they know it.

The new language recognizes what the voluntary world has known all along – that organizations are living communities with a common purpose, made up of free citizens with minds and values and rights of their own. From that language must grow a better understanding of organizations and of organizing, a new theory built on a new philosophy, a theory which has no need of words like 'manager' or 'managing' but which accepts that to be well organized is good, is satisfying and is a necessary pre-condition of effectiveness. Where better to grow that theory than in the seedbed of the voluntary organizations, which are ideologically ready for it?

The shape of the book

This book is an attempt to cull from what we know about organizations the skeleton of such a theory. It is therefore a book about organizations rather than a book about management – a word that should not appear here again. It is but a skeleton because every reader and every organization will want to put their own flesh and features on the bare bones, and also because skeletons take up less room. The bones are culled from a companion volume, *Understanding Organizations* (3rd edn, Penguin, 1985), which I wrote as a textbook for those making a more formal study of organizations. That book is a compendium of the most useful ideas to be found in research, with some examples of how they apply in practice. Anyone who wants to know more about any of the ideas discussed in this book is therefore referred to that companion volume.

This book sets out some of the things that are known about people in organizations and about the ways of organizations. The knowledge itself is common property and is neutral. It can be used by those who want to exploit others or, at least, to organize them for their own ends, but it is also there to be used by those who want to see their joint efforts produce the best results. It is as foolish to try to run things without this organizational understanding as it would be to go mountain climbing without the proper clothing and equipment. You might, of course, be lucky, but only the foolhardy and the arrogant leave it to luck.

The book is short. Busy people don't have time to read. There is more, much more, in *Understanding Organizations*, for any appetites that may be whetted. Evidence and examples have been put in the boxes so as not to interrupt the thread of the argument; they are not essential reading but are there to relate the concepts in the text to parts of the real world. References have been kept to a minimum, but the key sources are all listed at the back. *Understanding Organizations* has a whole section on the sources for those who would inquire further.

After this introductory chapter the book is in two parts. Part One deals with the ways of people, as individuals, in roles, in groups, influencing each other (everybody needs to know about this part). Part Two deals with organizing the organization, its cultures and structures and the chances of changing them (which is mostly for those who need to worry about such things).

The book is not a 'cookbook'. It holds few recipes for success. Don't look here for the quick organizational fix, or for the comfortable slogan. If, however, it helps you to think again about what you took for granted, to question the conventional and to trust your own intuitions, then it will have worked; for good books, like great art and great music, produce effects beyond themselves. And, at the end, don't keep this book. Burn it and write your own – for writing is thinking, and like the Irishman you can know what you think about many matters only when you hear what you say or see what you write!

PART ONE

People in Organizations

Introduction to Part One

Organizations are people. The observation is so obvious that it should not need saying. But too often we manage to make the people into neuters or ciphers in our concern for 'the organization', forgetting that each is an individual, that individuals run up against each other, that they have to work in groups most of the time if they are going to get things done and that, in the nature of things, some will have more power and influence than others.

I recall my first job in a large company. I was shown into a room which I would share with two others. On the door of the room were the names of the section and the department, in metal and screwed into the wood of the door. Below that metal plate were the slots with plastic slips, one for each of us with our name on it. It was quite clear what was temporary around there and what was permanent. Suddenly I knew the meaning of the term 'role occupant'.

You won't find many volunteer organizations talking of 'role occupants', but it is none the less important that they so organize themselves that people can work effectively. There are few things more frustrating than to be prevented from giving of your best in a cause you cherish because of the incompetence of the organization.

Organizational competence depends, to start with, on a proper understanding of how people think and behave, as

individuals, in roles, in groups and in relationships generally. Only then can things be so arranged that the organization enables people's efforts rather than getting in their
way. Part One therefore looks briefly at what is known
about the four areas of:

- the motivation of individuals (Chapter 2);
- people in their roles (Chapter 3);
- the ways of groups (Chapter 4); and
- power and influence (Chapter 5).

It tries to pick out of the morass of largely unreadable
research the necessary nuggets that can enlighten anyone
trying to make the organization more competent.

2

The Motivation of Individuals

'Motivate' is a strange word. It can in English be used transitively or intransitively; you can motivate someone else or be yourself highly motivated. Our ambivalence about how to use the word reflects our uncertainty about the subject, yet we know that in reality some things get us excited, energetic, enthusiastic, while others don't. We also know that what works for one person won't necessarily work for the next. Individuals are gloriously different but also in some respects quite similar.

Unless we know what it is that will release all the 'E' forces in an individual (where 'E' stands for excitement, energy, enthusiasm and effort) we cannot know how to create an environment where that person will work at his or her best, and we cannot know how to reward them suitably for their contribution. Should it be money, or more money, or is the cause enough? Perhaps responsibility is what they want or maybe more autonomy. It is this balance of energy contributed and expectations met that makes up what is called the psychological contract.

The contract works like this: into any situation, be it work, family or social group, we bring an unstated, often unconscious, psychological contract, never written down but nevertheless just like a formal contract in that we offer to give something of ourselves in return for something given to us. 'Motivation' happens when the contract is balanced.

When it's unbalanced, one side or the other feels cheated. Fair exchange is no robbery and breeds good feelings.

It is therefore rather important to understand what expectations each individual brings to the organization. One way of expressing this is to talk about the *needs* of the individual. There is a whole raft of theories about the needs of people

---

Box 2.1 The need theories

Maslow suggested that people's needs operate in an ascending hierarchy. Our most basic needs are physiological; satisfy these and we look for safety, then belonging, then esteem, then self-actualization. It is of no use talking of opportunities for self-fulfilment to an unemployed and homeless person who wants only shelter and an occupation.

Herzberg simplified this by dividing needs into two sorts: hygiene factors and motivating factors. Hygiene factors (food, security, sometimes money) are important only when they fall below what is adequate, then they demotivate rather than motivate. But to give someone more food when they've got enough does nothing for them. Of the motivating factors, however (like self-fulfilment, the opportunity for creativity and influence), you can never have enough. It is probable, although Herzberg doesn't say this, that one person's hygiene factor can be another's motivator and that different things work differently in different places.

Murray (and Roethlisberger and Dickson) extends Maslow and Herzberg by adding more needs, up to thirty in the case of Murray.

McClelland focuses on three needs: for achievement, power and affiliation. He has demonstrated that successful leaders have high needs for power and achievement without too much concern for affiliation. People with high needs for affiliation concentrate on relationships rather than the task.

Ardrey, after studying animal behaviour, selected identity, security and stimulation as his three key needs that have to be satisfied in one way or the other.

See further *Understanding Organizations*, p. 32.

– see Box 2.1. What they all agree about, if nothing else, is that different people have different mixes of needs, and that the mix can change.

Much nonsense has been written under each of these headings. Motivation has come to mean getting other people to want what you want them to want. Pigeons have been starved and then taught to dance for their food. To treat pigeons like that is distasteful; to do it to humans and then to dignify it with names like reinforcement theory is akin to calling murder a form of genetic weeding.

But there are nuggets of sense behind the nonsense. The idea of the psychological contract allows one to talk rationally about the expectations one has of oneself and of the organization and how to get them in balance. Role theory is not just about role occupants, it also helps to explain why relationships at work can be confusing and burdensome and may even lead to the phenomenon of 'burn-out', which too many voluntary organizations see as a sort of battle honour for good service. Groups don't have to be committees making horses into camels; they can be teams, teams which, research shows, can contribute more than the sum of their individual contributions combined. Finally, 'power' and 'influence' are not necessarily dirty words, daggers from the belt of Machiavelli, but an inevitable result of two or three people being gathered together for any purpose. To deny that people have power or influence among each other is to spit into the wind of reality; it comes back and hits you. Better to understand something of the nature of these concepts and to use the aspects of them that fit the values of the organizations.

Anyone looking for a further discussion of the underlying theories and research is referred to *Understanding Organizations*, which is itself only an anthology of the best.

Need theories, however, are dangerous. The implication behind them is that anyone who can satisfy the need has some influence over the behaviour of the person with the need. If I am broke and you have money to offer, then you are in a position to 'motivate' me to do something. It follows

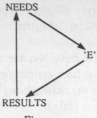

Figure 1

that if you want to influence behaviour it would be logical to create a need for whatever it is you have to offer. That way lies manipulation, enforced dependency and the more sinister interpretation of what management is.

You don't have to be a conspiracy theorist to see this exploitation of needs at work. In times of increasing uncertainty in employment 'job security' becomes a more prominent need for many people, more important than opportunities for self-fulfilment and participation or even, at times, than money. It is tempting for management, who alone can offer, even if they cannot guarantee, job security, to play just on this one need and let the others go unregarded for a while. 'Give them security and they'll be your slaves' is the way it can sound.

It is more optimistic to assume that human beings are more than need-satisfying animals, have indeed minds of their own which can distinguish between the long and the short term and between different needs and different outcomes. This is the notion of the individual motivation calculus, which operates the psychological contract. Each of us, all the time, does little sums, connecting the 'E' we have to expend, the expected result of that expenditure of effort or energy and how far it goes to satisfy something within us – see Figure 1. It sounds very simple and obvious – you do something if you believe that doing it will produce something else and that something else is part of what you want – but the implications are interesting.

For instance, if one part of that sequence goes wrong, the whole thing goes wrong. If you don't really believe that your action will produce the effect desired, then no matter how great the benefit or your need for it there will be no point in trying. Would you willingly work through the night addressing envelopes (effort) to raise money (result) to equip another centre (outcome) if you didn't believe that the money would ever be spent on that centre if it were raised?

The calculus is personal to each one of us. Nobody can do the sum accurately for anyone else. For one thing, nobody knows which of your many needs you will be seeking to satisfy with this action, or over what time span. One sign of maturity may be a longer time span for the calculus. Another sign may be greater importance attached to the so-called higher-order needs of self-fulfilment and people beyond oneself.

How do we know that this calculus works? There is a consistent set of research studies which shows that:

- People who are encouraged to set themselves specific targets (that is, to work out the calculus for a particular area of work) not only are much more committed to those goals but actually achieve them.
- People who achieve their goals set higher ones next time, and those who fail to meet them set lower ones (that is, when the calculus works well we push the sums up a notch or two).
- Continual success increases the desirability of the goal (that is, you persuade yourself that it really does meet an important need).

Consciously or out of habit, we operate this primitive calculus all the time: when we get out of bed in the morning, cook a meal or go to work. But the calculus operates within a different overall contract for each group we are in. There will be a different contract for the family, the organization and the tennis club. That contract could be:

- *coercive* – you are there because you have to be and you do what you are made to do (prisons, hospitals and some

schools, bits of armies and a few commercial organizations run on this assumption);

- *calculative* – you are there because you are paid to be
  there, in which case you won't do more than you have
  to unless you are paid more for it;
- *co-operative* – you are there because you agree with the
  goals of the organization and the people who work
  there, in which case you can't be *told* what to do but only
  be *asked*, because if you disagree you are quite entitled to
  refuse to do it.

Voluntary organizations should, by definition, operate
under co-operative psychological contracts, but it isn't
always easy to remember that this contract gives people the
right *not* to do something. Under pressure it is tempting for
those in charge to revert to a coercive or at least a calculative
contract in order to get things done the way they want them
as quickly as possible. Perhaps one reason why those in
charge of voluntary organizations can come to prefer working with paid staff than with volunteers is that a calculative
contract is much easier to operate. But even with paid staff
it would be rash to assume that this is the way *they* view the
contract. Even an employee of a voluntary organization is
likely to believe that they are working under a co-operative
contract.

To use MacGregor's famous distinction, a coercive contract suggests Theory X (people need to be pushed),
while a co-operative one is Theory Y (people push themselves). It is important to get the approach right.

The psychological contract is more subtle than has so far
been suggested. We are not just concerned with our needs,
we are concerned with the sort of people we are and who
we would like to be, with our self-concept. As Tolstoy
remarked, we tend to look for environments which bolster
the parts of us we are comfortable with, and do not then
want those environments to disappoint us. Holland, in Box
2.2, has a nice list of the different environments sought
by different types of people. Obviously it would be very

upsetting to someone entering a conventional world to find that it had changed to an artistic one, operating on quite different rules and principles.

Box 2.2 What is your preferred environment?

- *Realistic* – the realistic person seeks objective, concrete goals and tasks and likes to manipulate things. Such people are best suited by agriculture, engineering, outdoor work and practical jobs.
- *Intellectual* – ideas, words and symbols are important to these people, who are best suited to tasks requiring abstract and creative abilities, suggesting science, teaching or writing.
- *Social* – these people are best known for their interpersonal skills and interest in other people. Social work and counselling are possible jobs and so is the organization of others.
- *Conventional* – the conventional person copes with life by following the rules. Accounting, office work and administration suit them well.
- *Enterprising* – high energy, enthusiasm, dominance and impulsiveness are the hallmarks of these people, leading to occupations such as sales, politics, starting new enterprises or foreign service.
- *Artistic* – the artistic person uses feelings, intuitions and imagination to create forms and products, leading most obviously to the performing arts, writing, painting and music.

From John L. Holland, *Making Vocational Choices* (Prentice-Hall, 1973).

It has been suggested that most of us are continually seeking to increase our self-esteem and to enhance the concept that we have of ourselves. We do this by searching for psychological success, which we experience if:

- We set a challenging goal for ourselves.

- We determine our own methods of achieving that goal.
- The goal is relevant to our self-concept.
- We achieve the goal.

When these things happen we feel more competent, and the more competent we feel the more confidently we act. As Churchill said, 'We are all worms, but I am a glow-worm.' Of course, you have to feel that what was achieved was due to your efforts and not to chance. Vice versa, if you fail it is easier to accept if you can blame bad luck, another colleague or just the weather. Blaming something else allows your self-concept to stay undented. We ought perhaps to be kinder to people shifting the blame – they're only trying to preserve their identity so that it's there to fight another day. We also need to recognize that sometimes people don't try too hard at something in case they might fail – see Box 2.3 to understand this phenomenon.

Box 2.3 Play safe – be idle

A favourite way of protecting your self-concept in the case of failure is to claim, to yourself as well as to others, that you weren't really trying. You can then go on believing that if you had tried it would have been OK. This is called 'attribution theory'.

Instinctively we can and do anticipate this state of affairs. We don't try so that we can then genuinely plead that as an excuse.

Schoolchildren may well be protecting themselves from possible psychological damage in their examinations by not working or not revising. The answer, paradoxically perhaps, is to make failure less important even though the instinct of every parent and teacher faced with an apparently idle student is to underline how crucial the event will be.

We have ingenious ways of protecting our self-esteem, the neatest of which is called 'dissonance reduction', a form of automatic rationalization. It works like this:

We decide to do something, buy a car for instance. It is important that we convince ourselves that we bought the right car after the purchase and so we avidly collect all the favourable evidence we can, even reading the advertisements, and tune out any unfavourable evidence. That way we protect our concept of ourselves as sensible car buyers.

It gets more paradoxical. If we enrol on a course and stick it out to the bitter end we have to believe that it was a valuable experience, otherwise we should have walked out, shouldn't we? As a result any course which does not get 90 per cent favourable comments from its participants must have been truly awful.

Anything you join or do of your own free will, and continue with, has to be good, in your own eyes. Otherwise you have a 'dissonance' between your actions and the facts. Dissonance is psychologically uncomfortable, and so we change the facts, unless we have a good excuse.

In one experiment a group of students who were hostile to the local police were asked to write an essay praising the police and were paid to do so. Unknown to them, some were paid more (£5) than others (50p). Measured by attitude questionnaire before and after, those who had been paid less changed their views more in favour of the police; the others could say they were bribed, but no one changes their attitude for 50p, so to justify writing those essays that group genuinely changed their beliefs.

Voluntary groups inherit the legacy of dissonance reduction. No one can voluntarily stay in a group and disapprove of its ultimate aims and values. As a result there is much less criticism of the organization from within than you might find in other places. It doesn't mean that they are better, however, just that the self-concept is being protected by a bit of dissonance reduction.

Where does all this leave us? With a set of paradoxes:

- *Don't* tell people what to aim for; it's better if they work out their goals for themselves. *Do* emphasize that they must work out some precise goals against which they can measure success or progress.

Box 2.4 The appraisal trap

Conventional wisdom suggests that a good boss should tell his or her subordinates what he or she thinks of the year's work and give them pointers towards improvement.

This is well meant but hard to do. As individuals we do not like negative feedback. Our natural instinct is to find ways to reject it, and the ways are readily to hand. We can find fault with it, querying the evidence, disputing the relevance of the facts, arguing about its importance in the whole of our work. If that fails we can downgrade it in importance by persuading ourselves that the giver, the boss, is not that credible or does not deserve to be respected by us. Either way is preferable to having to adjust our self-concept downwards by a notch or two.

Paradoxically, praise is also discounted as a warm-up for the 'but . . .' statements or as politeness. To be accepted, feedback needs to be objective (observable facts), frequent and given by someone who is known to have a positive regard for you.

This is why second-hand compliments are so valued (because they must be genuine), why the sales figures for books are more telling evidence than reviewers' opinions, why washing-up can be pleasurable (we see the result immediately), why some social work is unrewarding (no easily observable results) and why running organizations can be frustrating (results take a long time to show).

- *Don't* shout at people who make mistakes; it will paradoxically make them try less hard. *Do* insist that they learn from the mistake and set new goals for next time; forgive the sinner but condemn the sin.
- *Don't* assume that everyone is like you; they may be there for quite other reasons. *Do* encourage people to

be explicit about their psychological contract, what they expect to give and what to get from their work.

- *Don't* give only negative feedback; it will diminish either people's self-concept or their view of you – see Box 2.4. *Do* find every excuse to praise work well done; stroking is good for the ego, and a good ego makes a good contract.
- *Don't* make promises for good work; it creates only dependent pigeons, and you will get locked into never-ending promises. *Do* make sure that people know when their work is good; are there obvious signs of success/progress which people can read for themselves?

For everyday purposes it is enough to remember these key points about the motivation of individuals:

- *People like targets.* Without something to aim for, work is just a job. The targets should be ones people have themselves accepted and therefore own as theirs; wherever possible they should be the sort of target people can see for themselves, so as not to be dependent on the views of others. Targets should be relatively short-term, or less than six months, else they are too far off to be real.
- *People like to feel good.* If you feel good in yourself you work better; you feel good when you succeed, that is, meet your targets, and are praised by people you respect. It is easier to raise someone's standards by raising their targets and praising any achievement than by reproaching them for faults.
- *People are different.* Different people want different things out of their life and their work, even different things at different times, or different things in different contexts. Check out the psychological contract if you can; it may not be what you think it is.

Box 2.5 The quest for a psychological contract

Dear Organization,

When I begin volunteering, please outline the following:

- What will I have to do?
- How much time have I to give?
- What do I do if something goes wrong?
- What training are you going to give me?
- After I have been volunteering for a while, will you encourage me to take the initiative in suggesting new ways of doing things?
- How will you build up and maintain my confidence?
- Will you help me to evaluate my skills?
- Is there a support group for volunteers?
- Will you let me know my limitations and when it is time to ask for help?
- Have you thought of advertising our services/skills more widely?
- If I am given more responsibility within the organization, how will you support me?
- If I get tired of what I'm doing, will you help me to leave gracefully or give me a new challenge?

Yours voluntarily . . .

The above letter is not from any particular volunteer to any particular organization; it is a piece of work to demonstrate what a volunteer could write to pave the way towards effective involvement.

The letter was written by a group of volunteer organizers who put themselves collectively into the volunteer's shoes as an exercise at a seminar run by Volunteer Development Scotland in conjunction with the Ettrick and Lauderdale Association of Voluntary Service.

From *Involve*, February 1985.

3

People in Their Roles

'What do you do?' The question, funnily enough, does not expect to be answered with a list of activities (writing letters, going to meetings, checking figures or even gardening, sleeping, eating and drinking). It expects the name of a role: secretary, chairperson, photographer and so on.

None of us like to be role occupants but none the less our lives are largely made up of a collection of roles, ranging from wife or husband, parent, supervisor or committee member through to friend, child or sister/brother. In fact, take away our roles and who are we? One of the dismaying discoveries of the newly redundant is that without a collection of roles we don't feel fully human. The obverse is also true; a bundle of roles makes us feel useful, needed and someone. It might even be true, in some cases, that we collect roles in order to escape from ourselves.

'When in doubt, man loses himself in activity,' an Indian guru once said to me, reminding me of Pascal's comment that all the unhappiness in the world is because a man cannot sit in a room alone.

No wonder, then, that organizations, perhaps particularly the organizations of the voluntary world, are peopled by role collectors. No wonder that there are overlapping roles, confused roles, ambiguous roles, conflicting roles, just too many roles per head.

Try drawing your 'role set' in your working role. The set

Figure 2

consists of all those people who interact with you in your job. They each have expectations of you, and you of them. It will be a star-shaped diagram like Figure 2.

If you wish to be sophisticated about it, you can vary the length of the lines (the shorter they are, the more frequent the interaction) and their thickness (the thicker they are, the more crucial the relationship). Even without such niceties you will be amazed at the number of lines. Is it possible that all those represented see your role the same way? Is it possible that you have an equally harmonious relationship with them all? If it is, you are lucky – and unusual.

Box 3.1 Role ambiguity

A number of vice-presidents in a variety of United States organizations were each asked to select an immediate subordinate whose work they knew well. They were requested to list the subordinate's major responsibilities, their priorities and the qualifications required for the job. The subordinates were then asked to do the same, for their own jobs. The agreement between each member of the pairs was of the order of 35 per cent.

From Maier, Read and Hoover, *Breakdowns in Boss–Subordinate Communication* (Foundation for Research on Human Behavior, 1959).

Can we be sure that it would be any better in voluntary organizations? Or would it perhaps be worse?

We need our roles, but they can be too much of a good thing. The most frequent causes of stress in organizations are: role conflict (two roles in conflict with each other, such as the caring person and the efficient supervisor, or the mother/worker clash); role ambiguity (when you don't know what is expected of you, or different people expect different things); role overload (just too many things expected of you); role confusion (when you are trying to be two or more roles at once); and even, unusual though it is in voluntary organizations, role underload (too little is expected of you).

A little stress is good for most of us – it keeps us stretched. But the stress that keeps us stretched is the stress of targets, deadlines and standards. The stress that comes from too many roles or too much role confusion is the stress that overloads; it may sometimes stimulate but it never stretches.

We can cope with the overload by:

- *Filtering* – screening out some of the complexity. We can refuse to deal with anything which isn't urgent (screening out the long-term), by putting problems and people into stereotyped boxes (screening out the unusual) or by tackling only those issues which need a snap answer or a yes/no decision (screening out complexity).
- *Withdrawal* – shielding oneself from some of the complexity. We can withdraw physically, by making it difficult for people to get access to us, with barriers of assistants, with a packed appointments schedule or by being continually in a motor car or 'out visiting'. We can also withdraw psychologically, reducing our commitment to the job and becoming uninterested, even apathetic, so that the problems begin to seem unimportant ('what does it matter anyway?'). 'Burn-out' is an extreme form of withdrawal.
- *Displacement* – unburdening oneself of the complexity. Alcohol, smoking, excessive eating, outbursts of irritation or even of laughter are all ways of letting out

some of the pressure, of simplifying the world again, for a short time. Without such 'escape valves' the complexity, bottled up within us, leads to breakdown, when we are forced to confess that we can no longer cope at all.

These coping methods work – for the individual. Busyness can keep the difficult problems at bay. Withdrawal can lead to detachment, while displacement makes it all easier to bear. Unfortunately one person's coping is another person's problem. The fact that I can ignore the long-term, the complex and the unwanted problems doesn't solve them. My escape valve is your mess to clear up. My frantic busyness is your growing inheritance of strategic issues.

Box 3.2 Research on overload

The role matters:
Margolies *et al.* examined a representative sample of 1,496 employed people. They found that work overload was significantly related to escapist drinking, absenteeism, low motivation, lowered self-esteem and an absence of suggestions to employers.

Kahn *et al.* found that men who suffered from role ambiguity experienced lower job satisfaction, higher job-related tension, greater futility and lower self-confidence.

The personality matters:
Friedman and Rosenham distinguished between Type A and Type B people. Type A people are competitive, achieving, impatient, restless, hyper-alert, feeling under the pressure of time and the challenge of responsibility. Type B people are more laid-back. A study in the USA revealed that Type A people between the ages of 39 and 49 had 6.5 times the incidence of coronary heart disease of Type B people. The same sort of results came from a study of Buddhist and Trappist monks!

It is naïve to imagine that there won't be role problems in

Figure 3

voluntary organizations. Precisely because their aims are often less than specific, because their organizational structures are fluid, because individuals are expected to shape their own roles, there is going to be, must be, more role ambiguity and complexity than in the more straightforward and structured organizations of business. If it is idiotic to think that role complexity doesn't exist it is also naïve to think that the individual will handle it positively by instinct, perseverance or just good common sense. It would be more sensible to help them put a little more thought into their roles and their role sets rather than leave it all to chance, character and serendipity.

It helps, strangely, to think of someone's, anyone's, job as a doughnut – or rather do'nut, because it is the American-style do'nut with a hole in the middle, only in this metaphor it is the hole which is filled in and the circle surrounding it which is empty (what you might call the 'inverse do'nut theory'). It looks like Figure 3.*

The point is that all jobs, if you think about them, have a core made up of things which you have to do if you don't want to be seen obviously to fail. There may well be a definition of these things written down somewhere, but even if it is unwritten it will, if you think about it, be clear about what the core consists of. It may actually be a rather basic set of things like keeping enough cash in the bank, or

* The 'do'nut theory' is extracted from Rosemary Stewart's work on managers' jobs, with its distinctions between demands, choices and constraints, and a diagram similar to the one above. See R. Stewart, *Choices for the Manager* (McGraw-Hill, 1983).

opening the doors every day, or seeing that the telephone is answered. The trouble is that even if you do everything on that list, whilst you won't have failed you won't have succeeded – because there is more.

The 'more' is the empty space of the do'nut. It is empty because it is unspecified. After all, if what it was were known, it would have been put into the core. It is the area for discretion, the chance for the individual to make a difference, to improve on the present. All interesting jobs have an area of discretion, an outer ring of space; those that don't are the boring jobs. But too much discretion is distracting for most people. We like to know the boundaries of the do'nut, how far we can go and where the edges of discretion lie. Jobs without edges are very burdensome.

To have the cure of all souls in a parish, for all hours and all days of the week, may be challenging but it is also never-ending. There is no time at which one can stand back and say 'I've done all I can' or 'I look at it and it is good'; for there is always more to be done, nor is there any respite from the role. The do'nut is infinite. That can't be wise.

The trick is to define your own and other people's do'nuts, so that:

- The core is well known and precisely determined.
- The boundaries of the whole are well understood in terms of responsibilities, time and function.
- There is enough but not too much room for discretion.
- There is a proper definition of what success or progress means within the role so that the discretion can be used for the right purposes.
- There is general agreement by those involved on the shape and scope of individual do'nuts.

Once do'nuts are established, it is possible to talk about two other aspects of roles in organizations which, unrecognized, can cause difficulties. They are: *role conditioning* and *territory*.

Role conditioning

People don't talk to people. Life is not that simple. People in roles talk to other people in roles. We see people from the windows of our roles dressed in clothes we give them because of their roles, and this inevitably affects the way we think of them, the way we behave and the way others behave.

Most obviously, using the language of transactional analysis, if we speak to someone using the tone of voice of a parent and treating them as a child we will usually get a child's response – maybe a docile child, maybe a rebellious child, but not a mature adult. 'Where are the car keys, dear?' can sound like a sensible adult, a complaining parent or a lost child, depending on which voice you use.

If you speak like a scolding parent, don't then be surprised if you get the response, 'How should I know? You had them last' (as from a child). Or if you speak like the plaintive child and it comes back, 'Now, just think. What did you do with them last night?' (as from a rebuking parent) instead of the adult response, 'I think I saw them on the kitchen table.'

Our perception of the two roles can condition the whole exchange and affect the whole relationship. Unfortunately, it is much harder to behave like a sensible adult than you might imagine – particularly if, in your heart of hearts, you don't think that the other person is quite as sensible or as adult as you.

Role conditioning has other angles – see Box 3.3. We can create self-fulfilling prophecies by the roles we (usually unasked and uninvited) put on people. Call a man a clown and a clown he begins to be. Every child knows how difficult it can be to escape from an early stereotype at school; once a trouble-maker always a trouble-maker in the school's eyes. It can be easier to change schools than to change perceptions of you in that role. Voluntary organizations aren't that much different from schools; for we all like to put people in boxes for convenience, boxes which become roles for us, and the roles become prisons.

It works both ways. Other people see us in our roles, not as us. That is often the way we want it. The nurse's uniform and the parson's collar ask us to see the role rather than the person, so that we can get on with the job, but we must not then complain that they don't notice the person. On a vacation job once, as a petrol-station attendant, I was much offended that my friends who passed by did not recognize me. I was invisible in my uniform. To the volunteer the invisible cloak of the role can be quite disorienting because they seem to lose their identity. After they get used to it they may welcome the protection of the role, for one of the hardest things to learn is how to be yourself in a professional role.

Many people find it easier to separate their private roles and their public roles so that there is some stability zone to which they can withdraw when the do'nut gets too much. For some, the organization and its roles may be the stability zone, their private roles the turbulent ones.

Box 3.3 Role-casting

Sometimes it helps to be a professor. For some reason people expect you to be honest, truthful and fair. Secretaries remember your title if not your name. Officials are prepared to see you. Bureaucracies answer your letters. Most of the time, however, the adjectives that come into people's minds are 'absent-minded', 'academic', 'impractical' and 'boring'. I like to think that the stereotype does not fit me, but the only way to find out is to drop the title and the role whenever I can. It is unfortunately one of the roles that carries its conditioning into private life.

Similarly, only more so, doctors are never off duty. Priests cannot stop being priests, even on their days off. Teachers are notorious, probably wrongly, for teaching over the dinner table, counsellors for counselling, politicians for politicizing every topic.

It is tempting to lose ourselves in our roles. Sometimes we never emerge.

Territory

All roles have a bit of territory connected with them. The territory is psychological not physical, although it may often include an office, a desk or just the kitchen sink. The point to remember is that we treat psychological territory as if it really were physical territory.

What is ours is ours. A stranger enters by invitation only and leaves when asked without, we hope, having rearranged the furniture, broken down the walls or in any way interfered with how things are done. The playwright Harold Pinter and others have built great dramas around the violation of personal space.

Our notional do'nut is akin to our home. It is our space. No one, not even the legal landlord, should intrude without permission, nor should we seek to intrude on other people's space without permission. 'Don't tell me how to do my job and I won't tell you how to do yours.'

This natural tendency to protect our psychological space is seldom openly acknowledged. Indeed, to voluntary organizations with an ideology which tends to favour co-operatives, community and sharing the very thought of a private role space is alien. None the less, most people treasure their do'nuts more than their desk, and organizations would be wise to recognize that and proceed by negotiation and discussion rather than by diktat when changing or checking roles.

Territory, after all, is ownership. And we care more deeply for what we own than for what we just use. Hire-car firms would thrive more abundantly if their customers treated their hired cars as if they were their own, and library books would last longer. So it is with ideas; if you want your idea to be acted upon, give it away, and then be glad when your colleague claims it as his or her invention! We are only human after all, and it is hard to give of your best to a temporary job at a temporary table in someone else's office. Part of the psychological contract for most of us is likely to be the chance to contribute in a role of our own.

Box 3.4 It is hard to say goodbye

Maureen had been promoted. Because the organization had grown so fast as a result of the new grant, a new layer had had to be created in the head office. Maureen was now supervisor of the regions where before she had been regional coordinator for London and the South-east.

What it actually meant was that they had squeezed another desk into the main office so that Maureen now sat alongside her replacement at the London desk. It was cramped and inconvenient, but Maureen was no stickler for protocol and anyway she expected to be busy, out and about, responding to the requests and needs of the regions. Strangely there weren't any. Instead there was a muted feeling of antagonism from her old regional colleagues who used to report directly to the director but now were supposed to answer to Maureen. It wasn't intended as personal antagonism but it felt that way.

Frustrated and suffering from role underload for a change, Maureen turned her attention to her old haunts, London and the South-east, where Jim, her replacement, obviously had a lot of learning to do. 'Let me deal with that,' Maureen would offer, hearing Jim on the phone, or 'I shouldn't do it like that if I were you,' or 'Would you like the background on that problem, Jim?'

It was even more hurtful to be told by Jim, 'No, thank you. I'll deal with this in my way.' After all, they used to be her desk, her problems, her baby. It felt like theft. It can be awful to lose your territory and to feel that you find a new one only by stealing it from your old friends.

An understanding not only of territory but of all the concepts of role is the key to a well-run place, be it family, office or national organization. We are all of us more than mere role occupants but we do occupy roles, and so do others. In our own interests, if we want to enjoy life, and in the interest of our organization, we ought to understand what is going on behind a lot of the words and symbols. What's going on, I'm afraid, is role games. They are part and parcel of life.

Box 3.5 Haloes and confusions

A well-known study (by Rosenthal and Jacobson) experimented with teachers' expectations of their students' performance. The teachers were told which 20 per cent of students had come out top on a test of academic potential. Those 20 per cent did better than the rest in intelligence exercises one year later. The thing was, the original 20 per cent were actually selected purely at random. The teachers' expectations did the rest. A halo creates a self-fulfilling prophecy.

Unfortunately the reverse is also true. Believe someone a dunce and they will often appear to live up to your belief.

We often try to act as we think others want us to act. But we may get it wrong, as in Laing's dilemma of the metametaperspective (!):

Direct perspective

John does not love Mary   Mary does not love John

But metaperspective

John thinks Mary loves   Mary thinks John loves her
him

And metametaperspective

John thinks that Mary   Mary thinks that John
thinks that he loves her   thinks that he loves her

Since neither John nor Mary wants to hurt the other, they get married. *Moral*: Don't act on metametaperspectives. Check it out.

4

The Ways of Groups

What is the difference between a team and a committee? 'A team is where you want to be; a committee is where you have to be,' said the inevitable cynic.

There is some truth in the cynicism. Teams are groups of people who are there with a shared and common purpose, each lending a particular piece of expertise towards a goal from which they all benefit if it is achieved. This applies whether it is a team on a sports field or a project team or an exploration team in Antarctica.

Committees are different. Committees are largely composed of people who are there as representatives of different constituencies, interests or sections. Committees are given different jobs to do from those teams are given. They are there to give approval to other people's proposals, to hear reports, to decide between options. They hold the accountability of an organization or of bits of it; that is, anything which the organization does is on behalf of others who are in some way represented on the committee. This does not only apply to management committees, it applies to the constituency committees of political parties, to boards of businesses, councils of learned societies, even the local church council and the Cabinet.

Committees have meetings, agendas and minutes, as a formal expression of this accountability. They are expected to reach agreement on the items put before them, an agreement which inevitably means the best compromise possible between the interests represented. A good committee meeting is one where all those present go along with the decisions taken, which does not mean that everyone gets everything they want.

It is tempting to try to turn committees into teams, with that common purpose, shared goal and individual contribution; tempting but unrealistic, because they are there for a different purpose, and some constituencies would feel that their rights and positions were being ignored if their representative was swept up into a cohesive team. A Cabinet that becomes a cohesive team is seen as being ideologically driven, stifling debate and rejecting dissidents.

It should not be tempting to turn a team into a committee. Yet that happens all too often, particularly in voluntary organizations, perhaps because the model of a committee and its ways of working is so ingrained in people's heads. So it is that task forces, working parties, project groups or local teams (note that the word 'committee' is often instinctively avoided) are often selected, not on the basis of individual competence but on the grounds that we ought to have a representative from the North-east, or from the unemployed; that agendas are prepared with minutes to be read and signed, 'matters arising' and 'any other business' duly taken in their proper order. The team has become a committee, and the meeting has become the focus of attention.

Teams need to meet, of course, but only as a means to an end. Everyone in a team knows that the real action takes place elsewhere and that the meeting is only a necessary interruption. For a committee, the meeting *is* the committee and is quite rightly the focus of the group. The team on the sports field will meet before and after to plan and review their play, but the time that really matters is out there on the pitch, where meetings have no place in well-regulated sports.

Most organizations need more teams and fewer committees. Most organizations end up with many committees and very few teams and, as a result, too many meetings, bloody meetings.

It isn't only committees and teams that matter. All work, other than that done by the lonely craft worker or creator, depends on people co-operating and collaborating in groups of some sort. They may be called gangs or sections rather than teams; or networks or clubs; or perhaps more informally 'my mates', 'the girls', 'Kate's mob', 'the boys in yellow' or 'that lot upstairs'.

Groups are not random. People in a pub or on a bus are not a group – until the bus gets marooned in the snow, and the people make themselves into a group with a common purpose, a way of working and a recognized membership. A common purpose and a recognized membership: these are the essentials, but the group will not be a working group until it has organized itself in some way and, usually, formed an outward and visible sign of its identity – a name, a place (territory), an emblem or a private language. Nor can a group be too big, for then it becomes a collective, an association or just a crowd, each with groups within it.

Groups have many purposes – see Box 4.1. They also get used by individuals for their own purposes:

- something to belong to, people to be with;
- a help towards establishing their self-concepts (you are who you go with);
- a means of support for their own work or aims;
- a way of sharing in something fun or worthwhile.

Nobody expects one group to perform all those functions or to be useful for all those purposes. After all, it is possible that the group doing something worthwhile is full of people you would never want to meet outside the office. We sensibly use different groups for different purposes.

But not as often as we should. Organizations are sometimes consumed with a sort of structural parsimony; they want to use the same group to do everything, from being the committee which gives approval to being the organization's think-tank and its oversight mechanism. It is a false economy. Even if the members are the same, the group needs to organize itself differently for each function, and desirably change its mix of membership. The management committee can change itself into a strategic think-tank but it will do it better if it goes away somewhere for a whole day, brings in one or two other people from the organization or outside and forgets about agendas, minutes and formality.

Box 4.1 The ten purposes of groups

Organizations use groups, teams or committees to do the following things.

- *For the distribution of work.* To bring together a set of skills, talents or responsibilities and allocate them to particular duties.
- *For the management and control of work.* To allow work to be organized and controlled by appropriate individuals with responsibility for a certain range of work.
- *For problem-solving and decision-taking.* To bring together people with the necessary capacities and responsibilities to deal with a problem.
- *For information processing.* To pass on decisions or information to those who need to know.
- *For collecting information and ideas.* To gather ideas, information and suggestions.
- *For testing and ratifying decisions.* To test the validity of a decision taken outside the group or to approve a decision.
- *For co-ordination and liaison.* To co-ordinate problems and tasks between functions or divisions.
- *For increased commitment and involvement.* To allow and encourage individuals to get involved in the plans and activities of the organization.
- *For negotiation or conflict resolution.* To resolve a dispute or argument between levels, divisions or functions.
- *For inquest or inquiry into the past.*

What is your group for? If it is meant to do all of these, it's suffering from overload. From *Understanding Organizations*, p. 156.

To put 'strategic vision' on the agenda as item no. 17 just before 'any other business' is one way to ensure that there won't be a strategic vision.

Groups, of course, don't always have to be formal. Informal networks, working relationships and loose alliances or friendships are the veins of an organization, where the formal structure is the skeleton. It is the veins not the bones which carry the blood. This chapter, however, focuses on the formal groups of the organization, because unless these work properly the skeleton is going to be a very oddly shaped and disabled body.

Even though groups are part and parcel of our everyday life, we don't always find them easy to be in or easy to run. This is at least partly because we don't understand their ways. What follows are some clues to this essential organizational animal – the formal group.

The starting position

Groups start off with a certain size, a mix of people and a task. These tend to be there to start with. This is often a pity, since with hindsight they might have been different, because we know something about the effects of each factor.

Size

Large groups allow a range of talent, skill and experience but also limit the amount of airtime or contribution that individuals can make. Small groups breed commitment and energy but lose out on breadth of knowledge. Which you go for depends whether you want expertise or commitment. It is said that good groups have numbers somewhere between the graces and the muses, that is between three and nine. Above nine and you've got a crowd, certainly a committee rather than a team. On the whole, it is best to keep any group as small as you dare.

People

A group must be large enough to have a mix not only of knowledge but of characteristics. The brightest individuals don't usually combine to make the brightest team. A group of like-minded friends may be too like-minded to be effective as a work group. If you want to get things done or problems solved you will be wise to find people different from you in their way of working but like you in their goals and values.

Belbin's research – Box 4.2 – provides the sort of checklist that few groups will ever match perfectly but all should strive towards, even if it means some people acting out of character on occasion. Note that the chairman is not the cleverest or the best at anything, except being the co-ordinator, leader and chair. Every group should at least make sure that there is one of its members primarily concerned with the *task* and someone who worries about the *process*, because one without the other won't work.

Task

Group factors of size and people, however, depend on what the task of the group is thought to be. If it is one of collecting information, then the more the better if not always the merrier. If the group has to be representative of all possible constituencies, then they will all have to be represented even if that makes the group too large to be anything more than a debating and voting assembly.

More mundanely the nature of the group's task affects the way it is run. A simple game shows this clearly. Take five people and arrange them in three different patterns:

- a wheel, with one person as the hub and the others at the end of four spokes, allowed to talk only to the hub, not to each other;
- a circle, with the five in a ring but allowed to talk only to their neighbours;

Box 4.2 Belbin's teams

Belbin has made a long study of the best mix of personal characteristics in a group, starting with his discovery of the Apollo syndrome – the finding that a team composed of the brightest people did not necessarily or even often end up as the brightest and the best.

He listed eight roles which are needed in a group. One person can sometimes do two, but rarely more. A group without someone doing each of these roles will perform below its best on most complex tasks or problems.

- *The chairman* – the co-ordinator. Disciplined, focused and balanced rather than brilliant or creative, he or she ís a good listener and a good judge.
- *The shaper* – the task leader. Full of drive, achievement and passion, he or she can be oversensitive and irritable but provides the spur to action.
- *The plant* – the ideas person. Introverted and quiet but intellectually dominant. Sensitive and easily hurt, he or she can also be careless of detail and may switch off.
- *The monitor–evaluator* – the critic. He or she has the ability to see the flaw in the argument, is analytically intelligent and often slightly less involved than the others.
- *The resource investigator* – the popular extrovert. The salesman, diplomat or liaison officer who brings new contacts and ideas to the group although he or she doesn't do much with them personally.
- *The company worker* – the practical organizer, who turns ideas into tasks, schedules and plans, an administrator rather than a leader.
- *The team worker* – the building force. He or she is uncompetitive but committed, likeable, good at listening and good at building bridges between people.
- *The finisher* – the one who worries about schedules, deadlines and completion. Without him or her the task might never be finished because people would always want to make it better or just to keep it going.

Abridged from R. M. Belbin, *Management Teams* (Heinemann, 1981).

- a web, with the five in a circle but able to talk to anyone in the circle.

Now give the three groups a bag of multicoloured marbles and ask them to sort them into four recognizable groups using only their permitted channels of communication. The results are predictable. The wheel gets the job done first because the hub decides the four categories and allocates one to each person to collect. The circle is always the last to finish, and the web is in between but usually produces a better-quality solution because more people have had more chance to contribute their ideas. Put pressure on the web, however, and it becomes a wheel as one member takes on the hub role. The circle never gets anywhere, because it is too hard to communicate, and no one can take the hub role.

The lesson is clear. If the task is straightforward or silly, like sorting marbles, then put someone in the middle and do what he or she says. That fails only if he or she is incompetent (which has been known, even when the games have been played as formal experiments). If the problem is complex and one mind is not enough, then start with the web but be prepared to change to a wheel when it gets to the action stage. Never use a circle, with people able to talk only to their neighbours.

If you want a quick committee meeting, run it like a wheel, with people speaking only at the invitation of the chair. If you want a good creative meeting, run it like a web but allow plenty of time. If you want nonsense, don't have a meeting at all, just let everyone talk to their neighbour in an endless circle. The point is, there is a choice; there is no one infallible rule for meetings or for groups. The task may be given, but the process is not.

The blend of size, people and task cannot but affect the way the group works. The overabundant research into the leadership of groups ends up by having more to say about the group than the leader. It confirms what common sense and the marble game would suggest, namely that:

- Groups which are committed to the task and believe themselves competent to do it can work in a participative, democratic manner.
- Where the task is not seen as important or interesting, some form of directive leadership works best.
- Directive leadership is also required where the members of the group feel unskilled or incompetent for that particular task.
- Small groups are easier to run in a participative way.

It is important, again, to remember that there is a choice. The voluntary world has an ideological preference for participative and democratic ways of working but then often ends up with necessary but unexciting tasks, large groups and involved but unskilled people – situations which cry out for structure and direction. With that sort of blend of size, people and task the result of a web type of working will be a lot of unnecessary time-wasting, talk and debate; inefficiency leading to frustration; a frustration heightened by the concern of the group members for the cause.

In groups, voluntary does not have to mean unstructured. Wise group leaders know this and vary their styles accordingly. But not all group leaders are so adept at blending the task, the individuals and the group into one. We all have our preferred ways of doing things if we are running a group – see Box 4.3 – and like to think it always works if only because of our combination of personality, acknowledged expertise and experience.

That, though we may not know it, is to rely too much on 'trait' theories of leadership, the belief that good leaders have what it takes, acquired from a mixture of birth and experience. Since nobody has ever been able to pin down the mysterious 'what it takes' (is it intelligence, height, self-confidence, enthusiasm, expertise, charm, sensitivity, insensitivity?), we would be wiser to try to adjust our behaviour along the participative/structuring dimension in line with the principles set out above.

Box 4.3 Roles and styles

John Hunt, in his research into leadership style, discovered some apparent inconsistencies.

Personnel managers were higher on the task-oriented dimension than on the human-relations dimension. On the other hand, welfare people scored higher on the consideration dimension, which may account for the criticism that they do not solve problems. First-line supervisors often turn out to be human-relations oriented but conceal it, in the belief that it is weak and feminine.

Successful women executives proved to be more task-oriented. In one females-only organization all the top executives preferred task-oriented roles. This produced endless struggles for power, much conflict and distress. The same was true of some hospitals, libraries and other organizations run largely by women. Do the human-relations oriented women leave the work-force, asks Hunt, or do such organizations promote only the task-oriented people? Nobody knows.

See J. Hunt, *Managing People at Work* (Pan, 1978), pp. 140 ff.

The life of the group

Groups have lives of their own. Like individuals they progress from infancy through adolescence to maturity. To use the mnemonic language of one study, they go through four stages:

- forming;
- storming;
- norming; and
- performing.

Everyone would like their group to start performing straight away, but that is only to invite a delayed adolescence. We do, apparently, need time in every new group to get to know each other and to make our mark (forming).

Sooner or later every person will speak or do something, but until that happens he or she won't feel psychologically part of the group. You have to allow time for that to happen if you are in charge of the group, even to encourage it to happen.

There is then the painful 'storming' stage when polite façades are dropped and people speak their mind. Sometimes the storm is within the group itself. Sometimes it is the whole group storming against the wider organization. Either way it is a sign that the group is coming to terms with itself and its task. Storming never feels good, to anyone, but it seems to be a necessary period of adolescence. Like adolescence it shouldn't provoke overreaction. It will pass and, once over, the group will start to decide how it is going to work (norming), when it meets, who does what and who can tell who what to do. Only then will they really start to perform. Needless to say no one wants to go through this process for a trivial task or an unimportant committee; but, vice versa, if they don't the task and the committee will remain unimportant.

Most groups have to take decisions. How they take those decisions is, as so often, a matter of choice, but as with so many matters of choice the choice matters; it should not become a matter of chance. Will it be:

- decision by authority;
- decision by majority;
- decision by consensus;
- decision by minority; or
- decision by no response?

The last two look odd but they happen. An idea is suggested, no one says anything, and it is dropped without any formal decision being taken. Or a minority bloc exercises its veto, and no further discussion takes place. It can happen that most decisions in a group are unnoticed negative decisions because they are not recognized as decisions. When this happens the group can become very frustrated and apathetic.

One of the key jobs of a chairperson or group leader is to:

- establish a procedure for taking decisions; and
- recognize a potential decision when it occurs.

The adroit chairperson will want to use consensus as the preferred method in order that all present will feel that they own the outcome. This is laudable but treacherous. Too many chairpersons establish what they think is the consensus but get it wrong. The group then hears it as decision by authority, which isn't the same thing at all. Consensus must be tested and if necessary reformulated and tested again.

Box 4.4 Are you group-centred or self-centred?

Do you genuinely:

- want to hear other people's ideas?
- encourage the quiet and the shy?
- feel prepared to compromise to reach a consensus?
- want to understand the reasons for any differences?
- want to share and express feelings, yours and theirs?
- feel willing to be challenged and argued with?
- try to clarify options and alternatives?
- try to check that everyone agrees with a decision?

Do you ever:

- use your personality to win an argument?
- form a sub-group of supporters?
- see the group as a battle to be won?
- withdraw, psychologically or physically, in anger or apathy?
- engage in personality combats?
- use the group as a stage for your own performance?
- act the fool?

There are two parts to the life of any group: the task and the quality of group life. Both are necessary in proper proportions. Too little emphasis on the way the group works will in the end undermine the work on the task; too much and the group may forget about the task and become an end itself. With the right mix of people and roles – see Box 4.2 – there shouldn't be any problem, but the right mix is not always there. When it isn't you will get more self-centred behaviour than group-centred actions, and the quality of life will noticeably diminish – see Box 4.4.

A good group is fun to work with and productive. It happens by choice more than by chance. There are things that one can do to make a bad group less bad if you understand that groups have a life of their own and are not just 'meetings'.

But groups can be seductive, too seductive at times. Small, cohesive groups at the top of organizations have on too many occasions produced the phenomenon known as 'group-think'. Group-think happens when a comfortable and cohesive group let their drive for consensus override their good sense when looking at all the options for the future. Janis, who invented the term, has described the symptoms:

- The members discuss only a few solutions and ignore other alternatives.
- They fail to examine the adverse consequences of their preferred solutions.
- They too quickly drop alternatives that at first appear unsatisfactory.
- They make little effort to get the advice of specialists.
- They fail to work out contingency plans for failure.

Too many organizations, even in the voluntary world, are run by a closed oligarchy. With the best of intentions these oligarchies can lead the institution down the road of the comfortable rather than the best. Janis quotes the Bay of Pigs fiasco as an example of a 'group-think' blunder, followed by the successful outcome to the Cuban missile crisis when President Kennedy had learned, painfully, that he needed to open up his decision-making clan.

Box 4.5 Group transformation

The director of the organization was having trouble with his executive committee, made up of his top department managers. They would not think strategically or long-term. 'Incapable' he called them and wished he could remove them. Investigation revealed that:

- The meetings of the committee always started with a review of past problems and performances. This 'inquest' forced the managers into departmental rather than company roles as each defended their territory.
- Decisions were by authority rule. Discussion was short and concerned only to point out departmental pitfalls.
- Agendas were long; time was short. The director wanted snappy meetings.
- The meetings were run on a wheel basis – all remarks were made to and from the chair.
- Two members of the group were not trusted or respected by their colleagues, although this had never been openly stated.

Changes were made:

- The committee was renamed and reorganized to exclude the unrespected members, so that there was more mutual trust and respect.
- The agendas were shortened, and different types of problem were grouped together. Bigger, longer-term problems were taken first not last.
- Meeting times were lengthened, and meetings were made more informal in their setting – the imitation boardroom table was removed.
- The meetings were run like a web, everyone speaking to everyone and the chairman summing up at the end.

The committee felt better, worked better, argued better and came up with better decisions. Everyone felt so, even those outside the group.

The ways to avoid group-think are clear: just do the opposite of the symptoms. Like so much of organizational life it is an easy discipline to state and a much harder one to practise. But some rules of thumb can help:

- Avoid any self-perpetuating mechanisms like the automatic re-election of committee members (which closes the membership of the group).
- Insist that all propositions to a senior committee, board or council come as a set of options with no specific recommendation (which frees everyone to discuss all possibilities).
- Every so often invite relevant outsiders to participate (which helps to break down any well-understood informal alliance or patterns of reaction in the group).

Groups are an essential and vital part of any organization. Everyone needs to understand how they work and how they can work better, and to walk that difficult line between making them too cosy and comfortable for effectiveness and too uncomfortable for efficiency. They should not be left to chance.

5

Power and Influence

At first sight this is a strange chapter to find in a book on voluntary organizations. If everyone is there because they want to be there, what need should there be for anyone to have power over another? The very words 'power and influence' carry suggestions of deviousness and deceit. Even if they don't suggest sin, they certainly imply hierarchy, which to many is almost as bad. Surely a committed organization should be able to rub along without talk of power and influence and the political games the words imply?

That is to think simplistically. Even in voluntary organizations these things happen – see Box 5.1. The words do have their respectable faces; the acceptable side of power is authority, of influence it is reason. When these don't work, we all find other ways of getting people to do something, even something they don't initially want to do. We may call those ways charm or persuasion, striking a bargain or making a promise, but they are still methods of influence, examples of power at work.

Consider this list:

- reason;
- friendliness;
- coalition;
- bargaining;
- assertiveness;

- higher authority; and
- sanctions.

They were the seven strategies of influence used by 360 managers in a survey in the USA, Australia and Britain and reported by Kipnis *et al.* in *Organizational Dynamics* (1984). Most of us have used most of these at home and at work at one time, and most of the time it has been sensible so to do; it has not seemed like an abuse of power, or playing political games, or even applying influence.

Box 5.1 Voluntary organizations talking

- 'We have found it difficult with regard to the attitude of the staff to have authority to run the hostel.'
- 'So far we've won; the power that rests with the professionals far outweighs the rest.'
- 'We have realized that he was more experienced and our suggestion was a wild idea.'
- 'We were told we couldn't have another staff member, so we said sod that, we'll get the money from somewhere.'
- 'Management committees, though generally composed of people in high-status occupations, frequently say they have relatively little influence on the organization of their hostels.'
- 'We have open warfare about rent arrears; the committee want them paid direct, we feel that would be a disaster.'

Quoted in C. Bennett, 'Powerless Management Committees?', *Management Development Unit Bulletin*, April 1983.

The truth is that if you have any responsibility or any role in a relationship you have to influence people and on occasion exercise your authority over them. Authority does not necessarily imply hierarchy. Put on a traffic warden's uniform, march to the middle of a crossroads and start directing the traffic. The cars will stop at your command because of the implied authority of your role. Take off the uniform, the outward symbol of the role, and you might have more problems stopping the traffic even if you were the commissioner of police or the Queen herself.

Anything can be abused, and certainly power is and can be used wrongly, negatively, for personal gain or selfish motives. All the more reason, therefore, for anyone who cares that organizations should be effective to understand how power can be used properly and how it is sometimes used improperly. Only with that understanding can one usefully look at contentious issues like democracy in organizations, the place of competition and the inevitability of conflict.

The sources of power

The language of power, like the language of motivation, is strange. There is, for instance, no verb that goes with the noun 'power' in English. If you want a verb you have to use words like 'force', 'make' and 'influence'. As soon as you use any of those words you are making a judgement; there is no unbiased language of power, which is part of our problem in talking about it. In this chapter 'power' will be the noun and 'influence' the verb; in other words, it will be understood that to influence someone you have to have some power.

That is not as simple as it sounds, as we will now see.

There are different sources of power. At its most primitive there is physical strength, or guns and other weapons. The voluntary sector is, on the whole, not going to be exposed to this sort of power, although those working in parts of the inner cities might not be so sure. There is, however, money, one aspect of *resource power* which is never far from the minds of any council or management committee. Control of money gives power to influence pay awards, new posts, promotions and expenditure budgets. Even in the voluntary sector, money talks.

After resource power there comes *position power*. This is the power that comes from one's role in the organization, a position on key committees or a member of the core group.

The role allows you, its holder, to ask for things, decide things, give permission or stop things. It is the most common sort of power in organizations.

Thirdly there is *expert power*: the power that comes from being an acknowledged expert in some area, wiser, more experienced or better qualified than others.

Fourthly there is an elusive type of power that can only be called *personal power*, because it is unique to the individual. To call it charisma would be to endow it with a false glamour, since it may be muted rather than star-studded, more about inner values and beliefs than about appearances – the sort of person one would go with because of who they are rather than what they know or have.

The different types of power come from different sources. Resource power and position power come from those above, or from those outside. Expert and personal power are given to you by those over whom you might expect to use that power. You can claim to be an expert or to have charisma, but the claim has no force unless it is supported by those who will be exposed to it.

No power counts as power unless it is credible and important to those who experience it. Money gives no power if money is not needed. The title of a role or a position means nothing if people don't accept the role and its responsibilities.

What counts as power in one place may not count in another. This can be confusing. The company boss who is master of all he surveys at work and comes home to find no one paying any attention to him is a standard feature of comedy. But the same applies to the volunteer who may be someone of considerable importance in his or her paid work and has to make a quick conversion to being ordinary as a volunteer.

The different power bases allow different methods of influence. If you are seen as an expert or as a personality then it is open to you to use persuasion or reason as a way of influencing people's actions or decisions. Of course, you can do this too if you have only position power – that is, a title of office manager or unit supervisor – but people are less likely to be convinced if they think you don't know much about the problem. In which case you may have to fall back on the authority of your position, expressed as assertiveness, on any rules that have been established and ultimately on obedience backed up by sanctions. Even these will not work unless your position power is backed by some access to resource power, in other words if people feel that you can actually sack them, cut their pay or their budget or increase their allowance.

Box 5.2 Power by invitation

Robert was a partner in a firm of chartered accountants, a man of substance in his world, a member of important committees, an adviser to governments. For him voluntary work was an escape from that world. He enjoyed his counselling, partly because of the anonymity it gave him. He was happily content to sit through committee meetings debating finance without once letting slip that he was an expert in that world. He did not want that sort of power in this world. He was not best pleased when the chairman discovered who he was and persuaded him to become treasurer.

Shirley was in public relations. Much of her day was occupied in promoting the causes of individuals and organizations she disapproved of. She was eager to put some of her time and talents to better use and joined the management committee of a couple of voluntary organizations in her community. Much to her frustration these organizations seemed less than eager to use her skills. 'If you are truly interested in these people,' they said to her, 'we would love your help in staffing the cafeteria at the centre at weekends.'

Expert power is by invitation only. Invitations are more likely to go to those who don't clamour for them. To be on the invitation list you may have first to establish your credentials as a member of that community.

If resource power is all you have (the position of many funding bodies which are not expert and not in authority), then you are confined to a process of bargaining and negotiation.

The study of 360 managers mentioned at the start of this chapter came to some interesting conclusions:

- The greater the power held by the manager, in terms of resources and position, the greater was the variety of methods of influence which they used.
- The greater the disparity in power between manager and subordinate, the more likely the manager was to be directive or assertive rather than to use persuasion, friendliness or reason.
- The managers relied mainly on reason to deal with their superiors, because their expertise was the only possible power base for them, looking upwards in the organizations.
- Friendliness was used when the managers had little power and little expectation of success and wanted to benefit the person rather than the organization.

These findings are depressing. They suggest that we find it easier to tell people what to do than to reason with them, and do so whenever we have enough of a power base to back up our words. We fall back on reason and friendliness when that's all we have going for us, rather than falling back on our formal authority when good sense and good talk have failed.

These particular findings were based on a study of managers in business. It would be comforting to think that it would be different in organizations with a different ideology. It may be so (there are no comparable studies). What is more likely is that the prevalent method of influence is affected by the size of the organization. In a small group where everyone knows everyone as an individual, the formal position or title counts for less; everyone has some control over resources; and so it is expertise and personality which count, with reason, persuasion and friendliness the accompanying methods of influence.

With size comes bureaucracy and therefore, almost inevitably, more impersonality, an increase in the part played by formal authority and a tendency to a directive style. Position power has to be the important thing in large organizations – see Box 5.3. So if one wants to avoid the more impersonal aspects of power and influence, it is best to keep the units small.

Box 5.3 Power in the public service

The bases of power were compared in three public service departments in the United States in 1962: a police department, a welfare office and an elementary school. Individuals were asked to state what authority was based on (some gave more than one answer):

	Police department	Welfare office	Elementary school
The authority of the government or governing body	27	43	35
The authority of position	63	95	60
The authority of competence	15	22	45
The authority of person	48	27	15

The bigger the bureaucracy, the bigger the part played by formal power (the welfare office was a statutory body). The more professional the activity, the bigger the influence of expert power (the school). The more direct the relationship with the public, the bigger the part played by personal power (the police).

There is one other way: the disciplined use of established rules and procedures. A team of surgeons and nurses can work efficiently and in almost total silence without necessarily knowing each other because it is laid down precisely what each should do and how the procedure works. Keep to the rules and there is no need for the personal exercise of power. The same is true of airline crews and good construction teams. Precise role description makes power unnecessary, unless things go very wrong. Discipline, in other words, paradoxically perhaps, is a way to get round the very real dilemmas of power in organizations.

The abuse of power

Power corrupts. Almost instinctively, and sometimes with the best of intentions, we gather unto us such power as we may so that we may the better influence the course of events. Consider some of the most frequent, and almost unnoticed, ways in which power can be collected and used in organizations, be they as small as a family or as large as a great national movement.

Negative power

We may all feel powerless at times to influence the course of events in a positive manner. Sometimes, indeed, there seems to be a power vacuum in our society because of this becoming modesty – see Box 5.4. But we all, no matter how humble, are in a position to exercise negative power. We may not be able to start something but we can almost certainly stop something, even if it is just the telephone ringing. The bureaucrat who sits on a file, the secretary who does not pass on a message, the janitor who turns off the central heating, the committee chairperson who won't call a meeting or take a decision – these are all flexing their muscles against the organization, often just to demonstrate that they are there and cannot be taken for granted.

Outbreaks of negative power in an organization are a symptom of something deeper. People, after all, do not exercise their negative power if they are committed to the organization, happy in their work, with enough responsibility to keep them busy. If these are lacking, if people do not know or do not agree with what the organization is doing, if they are bored or dissatisfied or if they feel they have inadequate responsibility, then it is that you will find them stopping something rather than starting it. If you want to take the temperature of an organization, look for the negative power.

Box 5.4 Modesty or vacuum?

St George's House, Windsor, initiated a series of consulta-
tions in the late 1970s on the subject of power and responsibility in society. Groups of influential people from different
sectors of society were invited to come to share their views
on who had power in modern society and whether their
perceived responsibility measured up to that power.

They came, sector by sector: the civil servants, followed
by the media, the unions, the managers, the politicians, the
financiers and so on. Each in turn disclaimed, quite genuinely,
any thought that they had power to influence events or the
direction of society. 'It is *they* who have it,' each said, but
each pointing in a different direction to another group, who
were only to disclaim it in their turn.

Each group saw themselves as having perhaps some
restraining influence but not a responsibility for leading nor
the power to do so. Was this cultural conditioning or a polite
form of modesty? Or was there at that time a general lack of
felt responsibility in society? 'Who', it was asked, 'are the
trustees of the future, if everyone denies both power and
responsibility?'

Gatekeeper power

Gatekeeper power can be used positively or negatively. It
needs to be understood because, like negative power, it can
be found all over the organization. Most of us are gatekeepers; we control access to information, as secretary to a
committee, as the society's expert on something or as the
group's representative on an outside body. We can hug that
information to ourselves, we can choose whom to give it to,
we can even lose it or forget it. Information is power, even
pseudo-information like gossip.

Gatekeepers know things instinctively. Even the best
intentioned of them need to be more deliberate and
thoughtful in their use of information, for 'open

government' isn't something that applies only to Westminster. All surveys of all organizations find people complaining that they do not know. Everyone likes to be in on secrets, but they wouldn't be secrets if everyone knew.

It is salutary to reflect on what information you have that others don't have. Why can't they have it? Because they don't need it? Who should be judge of that, you or they? Most information, when we get it, is unexciting, even unnecessary. Not having it is what arouses our interest.

Iatrogenic power

Ivan Illich is the great adversary of 'iatrogenesis' – the way doctors, for instance, may unconsciously or consciously induce people to think they have the illnesses which they can cure. The professions, argues Illich, depend on people feeling inadequate in the areas in which they are skilled. They therefore have a vested interest in de-skilling their clients. Consultants who constantly assured their organization clients that it was all common sense and that they had no need of outside help might be telling the truth but would also remain poor.

The iatrogenic tendency does not stop with the professions. All of us are guilty of it. We subconsciously want people to want what we have to give them, for that way we can influence them, by example if nothing else. It is of little use to have a fridge full of ice-cream if nobody wants it. We saw in Chapter 2 that need theory is an invitation to this sort of exploitation. Keep them hungry if it's food you've got on offer.

The worst of the iatrogenic temptations is fear. Machiavelli was keen on fear as a motivating device; better than love, he thought, because you can't control other people's love for you but you can control their fear. And fear works – in the short term. People will jump to it, if they're frightened, will keep things up to the mark for fear of punishment. But it is not self-sustaining behaviour; remove the fear and they no longer jump so fast or so high. Apart from any moral doubts we might have about the use of fear, in the long run it is expensive.

Box 5.5 Negative power

Pettigrew has listed some devices used to fend off an unwanted report:

- Straight rejection – the author and the report are dismissed out of hand. Can be done only with the backing of a lot of power and self-assurance.
- 'Bottom-drawer it' – the report is praised but then left unused. The author, grateful for the praise, may not press for implementation.
- Mobilizing political support – the executive calls on support from colleagues with similar interests.
- The nitty-gritty tactic – minor objections to fact or interpretation are raised to discredit and delay implementation.
- The emotional tactic – 'how can you do this to me . . . to my people?'
- 'But in the future . . .' – the report is fine for today but not tomorrow.
- The 'invisible man' tactic – no one is available for discussion when needed.
- 'Further investigation is required' – the report is sent back for more work.
- The scapegoat – someone else (such as 'the council') won't like it.
- Deflection – attention is directed to aspects of the report where people have enough expert knowledge to contradict it.

From A. Pettigrew, 'The Influence Process between Specialists and Executives', *Personnel Review*, 1974.

The issues of power

Because power is a forbidden topic in organizations, and particularly in voluntary organizations, there is seldom any proper discussion of two key aspects of organizational life:

the place of competition and/or conflict and the role or meaning of democracy at work. If they are talked about at all it is under the heading of organization politics, and in this context 'politics' is assumed to be bad.

Such myopia is misguided. Organizations are communities, societies in their own right. They cannot avoid the questions which beset all societies. Who has collective power? How regulated should competition be? How should conflict be handled? To push the issues under the table is not to solve them; to brandish grandiloquent slogans – 'we are all one family' or 'conflict has no place' – only outlaws discussion of the topic without adding to an understanding of it. If organizations are going to be effective social institutions, they need to grapple with these issues, which are not going to disappear as long as human beings live and work together.

Competition and conflict

Conditioned perhaps by British schooling – see Box 5.6 – we carry around an idea that competition is for most of us about losing. That is true only of closed competitions where only one or a few can win and the others lose, what one might call the horse-race concept of a competition. But competitions do not have to be like that; they can be more like marathons where everyone who finishes wins and in essence one is running against oneself. By introducing this new concept of winning, the organizers of marathons may have done more to change the culture of the West than they ever imagined.

Competition can degenerate into conflict, but that should not blind us to its good points:

- *Good competition excites us.* Why else do we play all those competitive games? It stimulates us to reach for new standards, to try new things, to learn new skills in order to prove to ourselves that we can do it; it enlarges our self-concept. In a team the energy released by the chance of competition is noticeable. NB: the cost of failure must not be high.

Box 5.6 Zero-sum games

The examination system in British schools has been norm-referenced for many years in most subjects. In essence this means that each year the examiners in each subject take the middle student's score as the benchmark for the year and relate the A, B, C, D and E grades to that. It is a well-intentioned attempt to be fair in subjects where it is hard to be precise as to what constitutes a pass. The effect, however, is to turn the examination into a closed competition in which a fixed percentage are bound to lose, even if everyone performs much better than the year before. It is not too surprising that many students feel that the cards are stacked against them and opt out.

The move towards criterion-referenced examinations, with previously agreed standards, turns the system into an open competition which everyone can, in principle, win – like music examinations, driving tests and swimming standards. How many people do you know who have not, in the end, 'won' their driving test?

- *Good competition sets standards.* One East European country deliberately builds two of everything even though one big plant would often be more economical, 'because by allowing them to compete they set their own standards for efficiency which we would otherwise never be able to work out theoretically'. Competition provides a basis for comparison. NB: the standards must be used not for punishment but for marking the scoring-line.

- *Good competition increases the cake.* By stimulating energies and raising standards, competition enlarges people's horizons, produces new ideas and encourages new possibilities, thus making it possible for more people (in a sense) to have more. It is closed competition, where the cake is fixed, which makes one person's gain another person's sacrifice.

For competition to be good, it must be:

- open – in that everyone can in some sense win, by improving their own performance and thus increasing the total cake;
- fair – in that everyone knows what the rules are, no one is specifically privileged or specially handicapped;
- forgiving – in that there is forgiveness for failure or mistakes, provided that one learns from them.

Conflict comes from bad competition, when, for example:

- the game is unclear (what is the objective of the organization, the purpose of all our trying?);
- the competition is closed (there is/are only so much money/people/time available);
- the rules are unclear (who is working for whom, and who gets the rewards?);
- the game is unfair (some individuals or groups get special treatment);
- there is no forgiveness (the price of failure deters people from committing themselves).

When one or more of these conditions apply, people start to fight each other rather than the world outside. All organizations need a purpose beyond themselves if they are to focus their energies externally. As all politicians know, a common enemy is the best douche for internal conflict, but an inspiring common goal is better still. It was St Augustine who said that the worst of sins was to be turned in on oneself. He was speaking of individuals but he might have been describing those organizations which have forgotten what they are about, where competition to make the cake has become competition to get the cake. It isn't just a pious platitude to say that organizations need to be very clear as to why they are there and what they are trying to do. With-

out that clarity, the competition will degenerate into conflict, with all its familiar symptoms.

Democracy

Voluntary organizations legally and logically are owned by
no one. Power resides with their members, or with their
clients as represented on the councils or management committees. Their constitutions require their governing bodies
to be elected in one way or another. In this sense they are
all democratic organizations, in which power belongs to the
people. Most of them are also democratic in their ideology,
distrusting hierarchies, vertical authority structures and
decision-making by small oligarchies.

For some it means that all decision-making is undertaken
by mandated representatives of the constituent groups of
the organization – voting by remote control.

For some it is a more conventional representative democracy in which representatives are elected and allowed to get
on with the decisions as they think fit for as long as their
team lasts.

For others it is a mix, depending on the type of problem,
with some decisions reserved for a referendum of all the
members, some for representatives, some for delegates.

Lastly, for others the democratic power lies in the right
of the members to choose their governors and to unseat
them at stated intervals if need be, leaving them then to get
on with the business of running the organization.

The organization needs to be clear what type of democracy it is working with. Direct democracy, however appealing in principle, is usually practical only with a small group
with a single simple task. Even then, in order for anything
to happen, individuals will need to have their own roles or
do'nuts, and to take decisions without consultation within
their area of responsibility.

These issues of democracy, participation and accountability are discussed again in Chapter 8. At this point it
is essential to recognize one thing, that if democracy is to

Box 5.7 Trust or control?

Trust and control are, as it were, placed in scales opposite each other. Put more emphasis or weight on trust, and control has to be lighter; more control, contrariwise, means less trust – see Figure 4.

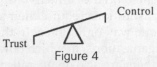

Figure 4

'It was her project, I told her, and I trusted her completely. The objectives had been agreed, the staffing and the financing. Now it was up to her, although I was always available if she wanted to talk to me.' One week went by, then two, then three. Still she had not been to talk.

' "What is going on?" I thought. "It may be a twelve-month project, but this lack of information is worrying. I must go and look, and I must clearly get some regular feedback, or the whole thing could get out of control without my being aware." 'I visited the project the next day, armed with a reporting schedule to be completed weekly and the idea for a co-ordinating committee to oversee the project.

'She was furious. "I thought you trusted me," she said, "but now it's clear you don't, else why these inspections and committees and reports? All these controls reek of distrust and occupy valuable time. If that's the way you want it, if that's what you think of my competence, I would rather you found someone else!" '

Did she protest too much? 'Was I wrong to trust her? Or was it my own insecurity which wanted the controls? One thing was sure, if I wanted her commitment I had to trust her, and trust her to tell me anything I needed to know. It seemed right; it certainly saved time and money; but could I risk it?'

work at all then someone in the end has to be trusted to get on with the job. Democracy does not mean, cannot mean, that everyone runs everything. It means, literally, that power comes from the people but that power is then entrusted temporarily to someone else, to be returned in due course *to* the people. If that sounds simple, even obvious, consider this: the more trust you give someone the less you should or can control them – see Box 5.7. Democracy, if it is to work, means, paradoxically, giving away some power for a time.

PART TWO

Organizing the Organization

Introduction to Part Two

Organizations do not, or should not, just happen. They grow, it is true, and they evolve, but from time to time people rightly seek to put some order into their ways of doing things, into their shape or into their systems. A form of social architecture is continually at work, even if at times it is more reminiscent of repairing the plumbing or building another shed on to the already interminable extension than of anything as deliberate as architecture.

History plays a larger part in the design of voluntary organizations than it does in more conventional bodies, which feel less compunction in obliterating the past once it has served its purpose. 'Ask the reason why something is the way it is,' said an American, 'and the British will always give you a historical explanation when an American would give you a functional one.' So it is in the voluntary sector. As a result, many voluntary organizations are lumbered with inherited cultures and traditions which may no longer be appropriate to the task in hand, and with structures and systems that would not be reinvented like that if they did not already exist. Like so much of Britain such organizations prefer, it seems, to stumble backwards into the future, a posture which allows them to keep their eyes and their longing fixed on the things of the past even while they move away from them.

Changing things is never easy, as we shall see. But an understanding of what could be and a perception of the consequences of different cultures and structures must be a useful beginning. Part Two is therefore a short guide to understanding:

- the cultures of organizations (Chapter 6);
- the structures of organizations (Chapter 7);
- the systems of organizations (Chapter 8); and
- the chances of change (Chapter 9).

6

The Cultures of Organizations

If organizations are communities, mini-societies, rather than machines, then it is natural to expect that each community will have its own taste and flavour, its own ways of doing things, its own habits and jargon, its own *culture*. No one would expect Merseyside to have the same culture as Bournemouth; both would be offended if it had.

It is surprising, then, that only in the last ten years or so has it come to be accepted that cultures can vary from one *organization* to another. This cultural blindness was probably another fall-out from the engineering model, which preferred to see organizations as essentially similar and essentially rational. One machine should be the same as the next, but not so one community and another.

To say that each organization has its own culture may be true but is hardly helpful. We need to put some order into the variety. One way of doing that is to look at the mix of organizational *styles*, each of which is based on a particular assumption about the ways organizations work. There seem to be four of these basic styles from which all organizations choose some mix, depending on their history, the kind of work they do and the kind of people who do it. Success is at least partly due to having the right mix at the right time. But because, as we noted in Chapter 1, everyone brings with them their own unconscious assumptions or ideas about organizing, the mix is often more a matter of chance than of choice.

This chapter should help to put choice before chance. There is a formal name for each culture, a picture and, for the whimsical, a patron deity, drawn from Ancient Greece. The point is that our fondness for a particular style or culture is often more a matter of faith than of logic, depending on what 'organizational idea' we grew up with or feel temperamentally in tune with. Here, then, is a brief description of each of the four basic cultures.

The club culture

The best picture to illustrate this kind of organization, the club culture, is a spider's web, because the key to the whole organization sits in the centre, surrounded by ever-widening circles of intimates and influence. The closer you are to the spider, the more influence you have. There are other lines in the web – the lines of responsibility, the functions of the organization – but the intimacy lines are the important ones, for this organization works like a club, a club built around its head.

Zeus, the king of the gods of Ancient Greece, is the patron deity, a very personal ruler with a habit of direct interventions, be it by shower of gold or thunderbolt.

The 'organizational idea' in the club culture is that the organization is there to extend the person of the head or, often, of the founder. If he or she could do everything personally, he or she would. It is because they can't that there has to be an organization at all. So the organization should be an extension of themselves, acting on their behalf, a club of like-minded people.

That can sound like a dictatorship, and some club cultures *are* dictatorships of the owner or founder, but at their best they are based on trust and communicate by a sort of telepathy, with everyone knowing each other's mind. They are very *personal* cultures, for the spiders preserve their freedom of manoeuvre by writing little down and preferring to talk to people, to sense their reactions and to infect them with their own (the spider's) enthusiasms and passions. If there are memoranda or minutes of meetings, they go from Gill to Joe or, more often, from set of initials to set of initials, rather than from job title to job title.

These cultures therefore are rich in personality. They abound with almost mythical stories and folklore from the past and can be very exciting places to work, *if* you belong to the club and share the values and beliefs of the spider. Their great strength is in their ability to respond immediately and intuitively to opportunities or crises because of the very short lines of communication and because of the centralization of power. Their danger lies in the dominance of the character of the central figure. Without a spider, the web is dead. If the spider is weak, corrupt, inept or picks the wrong people, the organization is also weak, corrupt, inept and badly staffed. Finding a new Zeus becomes a critical decision.

These cultures thrive where personality and speed of response are critical, in new business situations, in deals and brokerage transactions, in the artistic and theatrical worlds, in politics, guerrilla warfare and crisis situations, provided always that the leader is good – for they talk of leaders rather than managers in these cultures. They are a *convenient* way of running things (although not necessarily the best) when the core organization is small (under twenty people perhaps) and closely gathered together so that personal communication is easy. Once things get much bigger than that, formality has to be increased, and the personal, telepathic, empathetic style is frustrated.

The key to success is having the right people, who blend with the core team and can act on their own. So a lot of time is spent on selecting the right people and assessing whether they will fit in or not. It is no accident that some of the most successful club cultures have a nepotistic feel to them; they deliberately recruit people like themselves, even from the same family, so that the club remains a club. Zeus, after all, saw himself as the head of a family, and the same sort of feeling pervades these organizations at their best.

Box 6.1 A new Zeus in an old club

He came heralded by all – the charismatic spokesman for the oppressed people of the inner cities – to head up one of the big housing charities. An expert communicator, he was in demand everywhere and saw it as part of his job to raise the profile of the organization by his public appearances.

So he travelled – and ran the organization on Fridays. With a series of brisk meetings, crisp memos and tape-recorded messages to his secretary he raced through his week's in-tray and was off again to spread the word or argue with governments.

The world was impressed, but not the organization. Its members were not consulted. They hardly met this hero figure who was in their midst. They were dictated to, decided upon, budgeted with, without notice or say. They had been used to working in a collective, not a dictatorship. They rebelled.

He was furious. They were stupid, inadequate, ungrateful. His teams in the past had understood him and his priorities. They had done things his way in his absence. Why not here? Let them go and he would find his own team, his own club. The organization came to blows. He went, not them, and it was everyone's loss.

A Zeus needs a club – but it has to be his, or her, club.

The role culture

It is all very different in a role culture. Here the best picture is the kind of organization chart that all these organizations have. It looks like a pyramid of boxes. Inside each box is a job title with an individual's name in smaller type below, indicating who is currently the occupant of that box; but of course the box continues even if the individual departs.

The underlying 'organizational idea' is that organizations are sets of *roles* or job-boxes, joined together in a logical and orderly fashion so that together they discharge the work of the organization. The organization is a piece of construction engineering, with role piled on role and responsibility linked to responsibility. Individuals are 'role occupants' with job descriptions that effectively lay down the requirements of the role and its boundaries. From time to time the organization will rearrange the roles and their relationship to each other, as priorities change, and then reallocate the individuals to the roles.

The patron god is Apollo, god of harmony, of rules and of order. In best Apollonian tradition, logic and rationality hold sway.

Communications in these cultures are formalized, as are systems and procedures. The memoranda go from role to role (head of X department to deputy head) and are copied to roles, not individuals. The place abounds in procedures for every eventuality, in rules and handbooks. There are standards, quality controls and evaluation procedures.

It is all *managed* rather than led.

Most mature organizations have a lot of the role culture in them, because once an operation has settled down it can be routinized and, as it were, imprinted on the future. All organizations strive for predictability and certainty – for then fewer decisions are needed, everybody can get on with their job, the outcomes can be guaranteed and the inputs calculated. You know where you are and where you will be; it is secure and comfortable, even if it is at times too predictable to be exciting.

These role organizations thrive when they are doing a routine, stable and unchanging task, but they find it very hard to cope with change or with individual exceptions. If it's not in the rule book, they really have to wait for the rule book to be rewritten before they can act. Administrative organizations, as in part of the social security system, *have* to be role cultures and they will prove very frustrating if you turn out to be one of those individual exceptions. On the other hand, if the social security system were administered by a host of club cultures, each responding as they saw fit, social justice would hardly be served. Efficiency and fairness in routine tasks demand a role culture.

The important thing in these cultures is to get the logic of the design right, the flow of work and procedures. People are, in one sense, a less critical factor. They can be trained to fit the role. Indeed, role cultures do not want too much independence or initiative. Railways want train drivers to arrive on time, not five minutes early. Role cultures want 'role occupants', not individualists.

The task culture

The task culture evolved in response to the need for an organizational form that could respond to change in a less individualistic way than a club culture, and more speedily than a role culture.

The 'organizational idea' of this culture is that a group or team of talents and resources should be applied to a project, problem or task. In that way each task gets the treatment it requires – it does not have to be standardized across the organization. Also, the groups can be changed, disbanded or increased as the task changes.

A net, which can pull its cords this way and that and regroup at will, is the picture of this culture. Athena, goddess of war and patron of the commando leader Odysseus, is its deity, standing as she does for the task force and the problem-solver.

The task culture is the preferred culture of many competent people, because they work in groups, sharing both skills and responsibilities. They are constantly working on new challenges, since every task is different, and thus keep themselves developing and enthusiastic. It is usually a warm and friendly culture because it is built around co-operative groups of colleagues without much overt hierarchy. There are plans rather than procedures, reviews of progress rather than assessments of past performance. It is a forward-looking culture for a developing organization.

Task cultures thrive in situations where *problem-solving* is the job of the organization. Consultancy, advertising agencies, construction work, parts of journalism and the media, product development groups, surgical teams – any situation beyond the capacity of one person with minions to solve, and which cannot be embodied in procedures, needs a task culture.

The problem is that they are expensive. They use professional, competent people who spend quite a lot of time talking together in search of the right solution. You would not use a task culture to make a wheel, because the group would want to reinvent it, or at least improve on it, first. It is a questioning culture, which chafes at routines and the daily grind of 'administration' or 'repetitive chores'.

A task culture talks of 'co-ordinators' and 'team leaders' rather than 'managers'; it is full of budgets (which are plans) but short on job descriptions; it wants commitment and rewards success with more assignments. It promises excitement and challenge but not security of employment, because it cannot afford to employ people who do not continually meet new challenges successfully. Task cultures therefore tend to be full of young, energetic people developing and testing talents: people who are self-confident enough not to worry about long-term security, at least not yet!

The person culture

The person culture is very different from the previous three. The other three cultures put the organization's purposes first and then, in their different ways, harness the individual to this purpose. The person culture puts the individual first and makes the organization the resource for the individual's talents. The most obvious examples are those doctors who, for their own convenience, group themselves in a practice, barristers in chambers (a very minimal sort of organization), architects in partnerships, artists in a studio and perhaps professors in a faculty or scientists in a research laboratory.

Stars, loosely grouped in a cluster or constellation, are the image of a person culture. Dionysus is its god, god of wine and revels it is true, but more importantly the most existential of the gods, the one who puts the individual first, with all his or her talents and idiosyncrasies.

The 'organizational idea' behind this culture is that the individual talent is all-important and must be serviced by some sort of minimal organization. Person-culture people do not in fact like to use the word 'organization' but find all sorts of alternative words ('practice', 'chambers', 'partnership', 'faculty' and so on) instead. Nor do they talk of 'managers' but of 'secretaries', 'bursars', 'chief clerks' and so on, indeed, the 'managers' of these organizations are always lower in status than the professionals. You may have a 'senior partner' in a law office but if you ask for the 'manager' you are likely to be shown into the chief clerk.

The individual professionals in these organizations usually have 'tenure'. This means that the management not only is lower in status but has few if any formal means of control over the professionals. In a university, for these reasons, the head of department or dean of faculty is usually a rotating job, often seen as a necessary chore rather than a mark of distinction.

In other words, a person culture is very difficult to run in any ordinary way. The professionals have to be run on a very light rein; they can be persuaded but not commanded; influenced, cajoled or bargained with but not managed.

The culture works where the talent of the individual is what matters, which is why you find it in the old professions, the arts, some sports and some religions. Increasingly, however, some professions are finding that the problems are too complex for one individual's talents. Architects, city solicitors and even the clergy group themselves into task cultures and submit themselves to more organizational disciplines.

Box 6.2 The secret collective

Dionysians *can* run a service organization. After all, that is what professional partnerships do in law, architecture and medicine, and what community law centres do in the voluntary sector when they experiment with pay parity, self-servicing (lawyers doing their own clerical work) and group policy-making. Alan Stanton has argued (*Management Development Unit Bulletin*, July 1984) that there are many 'closet collectives' in voluntary organizations, self-managed teams working collectively but keeping quiet about it because it upsets the more managerially minded people in and around them. These are Dionysians turned Athenian in their pursuit of service delivery and efficiency, but hiding from the Apollonian cultures that could envelop them.

The mix of cultures

No organization is culturally pure, nor should it be. But our description of the cultures should help to explain why a person does not always fit neatly into the ways of an organization. Someone who has spent their formative years in the role culture will be incapacitated in the more intuitive, free-form atmosphere of a club culture, and vice versa.

Thus also role cultures, for example, find it very hard to change themselves into task cultures even if percipient leaders see that such a change is necessary. They often need a blood transfusion of new people if the culture is really going to change, and that, of course, is what tends to happen in the more cut-and-thrust world of business organizations. Where such dramatic transfusions are impossible, organizations tend to play around with the structure, partly to bring new people into prominence and partly to give themselves the freedom to set new norms of behaviour – that is, to introduce a new culture.

The mix that you end up with at any one time is influenced by the following factors.

Size

Large size and role cultures go together. The theorists are still arguing about which causes which. Is a bureaucracy a bureaucracy because it is large, because that is the only way to organize a thousand or more people, or is it large because it is a bureaucracy, because that is the only way to manage a complicated task and it has to be large to justify all the overheads of bureaucracy? Whichever way it goes, offices with more than 100 people have to follow Apollo to some degree.

Work flow

The way the work is organized has an important bearing on the culture you can operate. If it is organized in separate units or 'job shops' where a group or an individual can be responsible for the whole job, then club, task or person cultures can exist. But if the work flow is sequential or interdependent, in that one piece is tied in with another, then you need more systems, rules and regulations, and the culture shifts towards a role culture. In other words, a lot depends on what the job of the organization is seen to be. Specialization, for example, requires an interdependent and co-ordinated work plan and therefore a lot of Apollo, even if the specialists themselves are more in tune with Dionysus the individualist.

Environment

Every organization has to think about the raw material it receives and the products it turns out for society, whether those are bars of soap or educated human beings. If the environment does not give clear signals, if the institution is a monopoly and can therefore set its own goals and standards, or if the environment never changes, then the organization will tend to go for stability and a routine quiet life: a role culture. A changing or a demanding environment requires a culture that will respond to change: a task or a club culture. Precarious funding, for instance, will not suit Apollo, although a Zeus might find it a challenge and an opportunity.

History

Organizations are to some extent stuck with their past, with their reputation, the kind of people they hired years ago, their site and their traditions. These things take years if not decades to change.

You have to start with what you've got, which is perhaps the hardest lesson for enthusiastic leaders to learn, as they dream of what might be. A staff accustomed to a club culture with a strong central figure will find it very hard to adjust to the more participative task culture, even if they all claim that this is what they want. Old habits, particularly of dependence, die hard.

The cultural mix in any one organization depends on the relative importance of each of the above factors. Often you will find a role culture topped by a spider's web, with task-culture project groups round the edges and a few individuals of the person culture studded throughout like raisins in a cake. A consultancy group is different: a set of task cultures around a spider's web, with a very low-level role culture doing the logistics and the accounts. Other organizations are really a federation of 'barons', separate club cultures loosely linked together by a role culture, each free to run their own little empire.

What culture is your organization?

There is a short questionnaire at the back of this book which can be used to help you identify the prevalent culture in your organization, as well as your own cultural preferences. Most people find that they have one preferred culture and one 'back-up' one in which they are happy to operate if they have to. Most of us, however, find that one and sometimes two cultures are very alien. If those are the ones which prevail in your organization you are likely to be both unhappy and, often, ineffective.

To be imprisoned without knowing it in an alien culture can be very damaging to one's self-concept, and very demoralizing. Escape to a more compatible culture and one's skills, values and ways of doing things suddenly become appreciated; life takes on its bloom once more. It's like a happy marriage. 'Cultural fit' is a much-neglected element in morale and motivation.

Because of their history and traditions, voluntary organizations are peculiarly prone to cultural confusion. As we saw in Chapter 1, there are different types of voluntary organization: the mutual-support organization, the service organization and the campaigning organization, with many voluntary bodies deliberately or accidentally combining all three. The three types have distinct cultural preferences. The mutual-support organization is instinctively Dionysian, of the person culture. It is not, of course, akin to a barristers' chambers or a university, in that the individuals would not claim to be stars. But they *are* there, in that organization, as *individuals*, with the right to stay as long as they like, under a pure 'co-operative' psychological contract, seeing themselves as servant to no one and employed by no one.

Such groups will not want to be 'managed' or to have such people as 'managers', but will have branch 'secretaries', area 'co-ordinators' and national 'conferences'. The officers of the society will be very much the servants of the members, for it is the members who are the whole point and purpose of the organization, just as a partnership cannot exist without its partners. In such a culture no one can give orders, lay down rules or impose disciplines; the very words are alien to the culture. Instead there is organization by consent, agreement on procedures, participation and full democracy in which one person's voice is in theory as good as another's.

That won't work in a service organization. Service organizations have a job to do, standards to keep up, accountabilities to clients and to funders. They cannot accept *anyone* who wants to join, nor can they tolerate substandard performance. Where there are volunteer operators they are carefully selected and well trained, in fact equivalent to employed staff without the salary.

Such organizations often prefer to work with as many paid professional staff as they can afford, because this gives them more control and predictability in delivery of their service. In other words, their task pulls them towards the Apollonian role culture, with its job descriptions, authority ranking, systems and rules. In these organizations the volunteer is more often found on the fringes, helping to raise money and support, providing ancillary services such as transport or safeguarding the public accountability of the organization by sitting on its council or management committee.

Apollo has a much lesser and lower role to play in the third category, the campaigning organization. Such organizations need an efficient office to serve the campaign. But the key figure will nearly always be a Zeus by inclination

Box 6.3 Apollo into Dionysus won't go

He became a priest in his forties, after a successful career as an accountant in an engineering firm. Gradually he had felt the need to contribute his skills and his energies to the thing that mattered most to him – his religion. After ordination and a brief curacy he was appointed to a large suburban parish in the Midlands. As churches go it was quite thriving, with reasonable congregations on Sundays and a cluster of little groups and committees on everything from Bible study to marriage preparation.

As he looked at it, however, it reeked of inefficiency. There was no proper reporting system; there were no clear goals or targets; no one was really accountable for anything; it was all talk and very little performance. He saw a clear opportunity to apply his past skills and training and devise a proper organization.

The committees and groups were dissolved. The work was divided into 'divisions', each with its own budget and divisional officer, who was in turn in charge of a number of project officers. There was a Finance Division, a Pastoral Division, an Educational Division and so on. Applications were invited for these (unpaid) roles, job descriptions were circulated and interviews scheduled.

To his surprise few candidates applied, and those who did so were quite unsuitable, so much so that he felt he couldn't even offer them a proper interview. More hurtful were the letters he received from many stalwarts of the congregation accusing him of assuming dictatorial powers, of arrogantly denigrating all the good work of the past. Then the church-wardens resigned. They appreciated his sincerity, they said, but this was, after all, a congregation not a business. People had a right to offer their talents in the way they wanted to. He was asking people to assume responsibility for other people when what they wanted to do was to 'serve'. They themselves, they said, were the guardians of the people not their masters.

Hurt and puzzled he backed down, but not before he had accused them all from his pulpit of being more interested in 'being' than 'doing', in serving themselves than in serving others. His theology may have been right, but his organizational approach was not. A Dionysian mutual-support organization cannot be turned into a service organization overnight by Apollonian decrees.

and temperament, who will become and be seen as the personal embodiment of the organization, who will lead rather than manage the campaign. Zeus, however, may well be supported by small task forces tackling special issues, problem-solvers in the co-operative Athenian or task-culture role, people who may be volunteers or who may be paid. It is the way they organize themselves that matters here, not their status.

Each culture is appropriate in its place. The problems come when you mix them. Dionysians find it particularly hard to tolerate the necessary restrictions and formalities of the Apollonian role culture. Apollonians are uncomfortable in the more buccaneering world of Zeus with its higher profiles and higher risks. Athenians can tolerate an effective Zeus and talented Dionysian experts but, again, chafe at the bureaucracy, as they see it, of the role culture. When a mutual-support group, proper Dionysians all, decide to set up their own educational or care-providing agency, they have to import Apollo, to start having paid staff, some of whom may not share all the idealism of the original founders; for, as they see it, they are paid to do a job, a straightforward economic contract. The value clashes of voluntary organizations are sometimes more truthfully a clash of cultures, of different organizational ideas.

There is no simple solution to the problems of a cultural mix. Any organization of any complexity will have them. This is why anyone who was in at the birth of an organization will always remember it wistfully, because, despite all the haste and all the crises, there was a simplicity about the early days which allowed one culture to flourish, one set of values to envelop everything. Success often brings complexity and a need for the other cultures. To exclude or ignore them is to put the organization itself at risk.

The first lesson, once again, is that it is OK to be different. The other cultures are perfectly respectable and viable ways of running things, even if they aren't your ways. In particular it helps to remember that:

- *Zeus people are personalities*. They relate to other personalities and think in terms of individuals. In the club culture, organizational changes are made by switching key people around or by bringing in new people from outside. Zeus people have fat address books, cultivate networks and are intolerant of forms, bits of paper and systems. Ask a Zeus person to draw you a picture of the organization and you will get something that looks like the solar system studded with the names of the key people.

- *Apollo people are logical people*. They like things to be done rationally and formally. If changes are needed they will instinctively want to change the structure or the procedures, believing that it is the logic rather than the people which needs to be altered. They tolerate, even enjoy, committees, seeing them as a rational way to sort out problems. They appreciate routine and like to have everything if not under control then at least predictable. It is Apollonians who keep the organization going when everyone else is off doing their thing. They are the ones who know the constitution of the organization by heart and invoke it whenever Zeus tramples over its fences.

- *Athenians enjoy problems and teams*. They are often strivers for perfection, not necessarily in an ambitious way but because they believe that problems should be solved *well*, not just disposed of. They are gregarious in that they enjoy working with other competent people and they enjoy working hard. On the other hand, they are bored by the trivial, the mundane and the repetitive, which provide no challenge to their problem-solving capacities. They are great people when new projects have to be started, new products developed, new crises faced, but would hate to be administrators or desk-bound all day answering the telephone. Athenians change things by redefining the task and then regrouping the teams.

- *Dionysians do not really belong in organizations at all*, although necessarily many end up there as a way of getting paid. They are loners but, unlike Zeus people, they do not covet power, only respect and influence. Zeus people, interestingly, often think of themselves as Dionysians, pretending to themselves that power does not concern them – although their colleagues might not agree! True Dionysians value freedom highly, the right to make their own decisions, to work in their own way and to express their own identities; they like to think of no one as their boss.

To accept the differences between the cultures is the first step to understanding. Understanding and mutual tolerance aren't enough to make an effective organization but they are a good beginning.

The second lesson from the story of the cultures is the reminder that the most effective organizations have a mix of cultures attuned to their individual circumstances – what might be called the theory of cultural propriety. As organizations grow, it is easy for the balance to get out of tune.

Organizations usually start with an enthusiastic Zeus and an accompanying club, or a band of committed Dionysians. Size demands that they complement this culture with some features of an Apollonian role culture whose formalities are alien to Zeus and Dionysus. Many organizations cannot take this step; they remain small and marginal rather than change their ethos and their culture. Apollo, however, can fossilize in time. To keep the organization relevant and successful, the new mixed culture needs to have some Athenian projects and task cultures dotted through it, something not always easy for Zeus or Apollo to recognize and accept.

Rebalancing the mix of cultures is never easy but always necessary. It can't be left to chance and time because it involves changing how things are done and even the people who do them. Wise organizations understand that their culture is never set in stone.

Box 6.4 Guess the god

Try this game.

Ask someone what their job is.

If they reply, 'I work for X' (naming a person), then they are probably in a Zeus club culture.

If they reply, 'I work for X organization', they probably belong to an Apollo role culture.

If they reply, 'I am a Y in X organization', then they think of themselves as a professional in an organization, i.e. part of an Athenian task culture.

If they reply, 'I am a writer' (or architect and so on), they are likely to be a Dionysian.

Or look at the telephone list in an organization. If it has only the names of the staff, then it is either a club culture or a bunch of Dionysians. If the job titles or the departments come first, then it is Apollo-dominated.

7

The Structures of Organizations

'Who needs a structure? Structures are prisons.' The speaker, naturally, was a Dionysian but was airing a view that is often expressed in parts of the voluntary sector. Yet it would be naïve to think that any organization, even a family, can work well without some way of dividing up the work to be done, without some understanding of accountability, of who is accountable to whom for what, and without some agreement on the general shape of the organization, whether it is to be an alliance of independent groups or one big machine. Without a division of work, a system of accountability and a coherent shape to the organization, there are bits of work that don't get done, messages which don't get heard, decisions made by accident, with irritation and confusion in abundance.

It is better to look at the structure of an organization as its skeleton, not its prison, a skeleton which does not come alive until there are people and groups and tasks to get the blood running and the nerves and sinews working. In the voluntary sector, these structures have to take particular account of the co-operative nature of the psychological contract; voluntary organizations need to be as informal as possible, as participative as is practical and, in their shape, the flatter the better.

In this chapter we look briefly at:

- the shape of the job;

- the shape of the structure; and
- the shape of the organization.

Box 7.1 When organizing goes wrong

Professor John Child has compiled a depressing but impress-. ive list of the things that can be wrong if the work of the organization is not properly designed and structured. Here is just part of his list:

- Movitation and morale may be depressed because:
  – Decisions appear to be inconsistent and arbitrary in the absence of standardized rules.
  – People believe that they have little responsibility, opportunity for achievement and recognition of their worth because of insufficient delegation.
  – There is a lack of clarity as to what is expected of people and how their performance is assessed.

- Decision-making may be delayed and lacking in quality because:
  – Necessary information is not transmitted on time to the appropriate people.
  – Decision-makers are overloaded due to insufficient delegation.
  – There are no adequate procedures for evaluating the results of similar decisions in the past.

- There may be conflict and a lack of co-ordination because:
  – There are conflicting goals between projects and departments.
  – Mechanisms for liaison have not been laid down.
  – The people involved in operations are not involved in the planning.

- Costs may be rising rapidly because:
  – The organization has a long hierarchy with a high ratio of 'chiefs' to 'indians'.
  – There is an excess of procedures and paperwork.

For the complete list see J. Child, *Organization: A Guide to Problems and Practice* (Harper & Row, 1984).

In so doing we will reach for an understanding of how the

design of an organization can dramatically help or dangerously hinder the work which it is trying to do. We neglect it at our peril – see Box 7.1.

The shape of the job

Voluntary organizations ought to believe in and practise subsidiarity. Subsidiarity is actually part of the teaching of the Roman Catholic Church, which holds it to be a moral principle that a higher-order body should not do things which a lower-order body could do perfectly well. In other words, give people as much responsibility as they can handle. To do anything else is in a sense to steal people's choices from them; and since most people in a voluntary organization are there because they believe in the work, they will want as much of that work as they can reasonably handle. In the analogy of Chapter 3, voluntary organizations should aim to work with large do'nuts.

It is important to remember this, because there are many pressures in organizations which push them towards smaller jobs or what has been called the micro-division of labour. Consider:

- If jobs are broken down into their smallest elements, unskilled people can do them with little training. Not everyone is capable of handling a large do'nut. Not everyone wants to.
- If jobs are broken down and training times are short, then the work-force becomes more interchangeable. No one is indispensable for long. The work does not get held up because one person is missing.
- If jobs are standardized, then quality is easier to predict and to monitor. Someone doing only one job will soon learn to be an expert, which is less likely to happen if their time is spread out over a variety of jobs.

On the other hand, we know that:

- Small, boring jobs breed fatigue, distraction and accidents, whereas moderately complicated tasks generate

psychological impulses towards their own completion, and an in-built kind of traction.
- People, unlike machines, work more efficiently at a variable than at a constant rate.
  When work is minutely subdivided, the worker feels it to be some reflection on himself or herself. It is hard to identify the individual contribution in the end product, hard to see how one has personally made a difference.

Too often the first list gets higher priority than the second list, or one small boring job is added to another and called job enlargement. Voluntary organizations can often appear self-exploiting, giving their members, who are often very capable individuals, menial jobs to do on the implicit understanding that one will readily do for nothing things that no one would want to do for money. Menial and boring jobs have to be done, although many can and should be automated, but they are more tolerable if they are done in short bursts and as part of something bigger. One cannot rely on idealism forever cancelling out the negative effects of the micro-division of labour – see Box 7.2.

That is why many organizations are moving to the concept of job shops, whereby a group of workers are responsible for a whole sequence of operations, which might be the assembly of a product, or the preparation and dispatch of a broadsheet, or the planning and delivery of a new campaign. The members of the group can then share the work out amongst themselves, rotating the least desirable parts as one of the necessary but shared chores. Wise families rotate the chores. So do wise groups.

The shape of the structure

All organizations have to live with the conflicting principles of *diversity* and *uniformity*. All organizations would like to operate in a quiet and totally predictable world. That way everything could be perfect, Apollo triumphant. Unfortunately the world doesn't work that way. It is full of uncertainty and differences, and any organization which doesn't recognize that and accommodate itself to it will not, in the end, survive.

Box 7.2 The Findhorn way

At Findhorn in the North of Scotland there live and work a special community of people. In that community all are equal and all work, paying themselves only a few pounds a week as pocket-money. They seek to be a model community but they pay their way by being also a place of learning and education. As a community, they put on a large number of courses and 'experience weeks' to enable people to experience and understand some part of what they believe and how they live.

As a result there is a wide range of jobs to be done, ranging from sophisticated publishing and photography, and skilled educational leadership roles, down to the chores of sweeping the roads, cleaning the toilets and writing the cheques. Everyone does his or her turn at the chore tasks, which are not seen as menial so much as necessary. But because no one does them for ever, and because they are treated as of equal worth, no one is intended to see them as personally demeaning; they are part of something bigger.

The Findhorn community has sought after a new philosophy of organizing, one in which groups do not have leaders but 'focalizers' as a sign of their desire to avoid hierarchy; where all work is equally valued; and where the wealth of the community is social property belonging to the whole rather than to individuals.

Could voluntary organizations do the same? Some try to, but without the all-absorbing environment of Findhorn they can end up demanding too much in relation to what they can offer. A cause is not the same as a whole life-support system, and even at Findhorn most people leave after three or four years.

Small groups can, however, often achieve what whole organizations could not carry off. There are many community projects where the Findhorn principles are practised – but again, longevity is not always their most noticeable feature.

What organizations do, if you watch them, is match their structure to the major points of diversity and then try to hold the whole thing together. In business, if the organization has some very different products (as different, maybe, as chalk and cheese), then it will soon develop a chalk division and a cheese division. If on the other hand it sells only chalk, then it will find that the major differences lie in its customers and it may create a 'schools' division and a 'domestic' division representing two very different types of market. Alternatively, if Scotland's chalk habits are very different from those of Wales, it may create a regional structure. In addition, the organization will probably have kept its functional division of production, finance, personnel and marketing.

Big companies can often end up with all four in a complicated quadrilateral matrix structure, so that you have to be clear that you are a *personnel* officer involved in making *chalk* for *schools* in *Scotland*.

Voluntary organizations tend to see themselves as single-product businesses with clients differentiated regionally. That is the way their history has developed. But if they sit back and look at themselves they may see more than one 'product' or 'service', and it may make more sense to think of the occupational categories of their clients rather than where they live. A fund-raising organization for the developing world, for instance, may decide that it is providing education as well as raising money and may need to *recognize the difference* in its structure by creating an educational division to augment its money-collecting activity. It may be more sensible to have, in the educational division, someone responsible for all schools and someone else for the media, rather than dividing it between North and South.

Divisional organization is not a precise art, which is why the structures of organizations keep switching and flexing. This is not a case of the people at the top being unable to make up their minds, or wanting to change offices, or playing power games (although these things happen in the best-regulated organization), but a natural response to a *changing pattern of diversity*. Some organizations revel in diversity and cultivate it – see Box 7.3 – but they often run into problems when they try to pick up the pieces. Apple Computers grew apace by giving each product total independence, only to come perilously close to bankruptcy when they discovered that no one was in a sense minding the house whilst the family was playing. Uniformity was swamped by diversity.

Box 7.3 The new words for organizations

Which of these describes your organization?

- *Adhocracy* – a shifting scene where job titles change from week to week, jobs are transformed, responsibilities shift, structures are dismantled and reassembled.
- *Tents* – the opposite to palaces, temporary groupings with imprecise objectives, geared to experiment.
- *The technology of foolishness* – individuals and organizations need ways of doing things for which they have no good reason; it aids inventiveness.
- *Loosely coupled* – organizations need constant experiment; 'retrospective sense-making' is the key to success by choosing from a large number of experiments.
- *Garbage-can* – organizations should not be expected to be models of rationality; a bit of mess isn't necessarily bad.
- *Market-place* – rather than planning everything, some organizations work on the principle of the survival of the fittest and encourage internal competition.
- *Champions*, *bootleggers*, *skunk works*, *cabals* and *shadow organizations* – some of the words describing internal entrepreneurs.
- *Networks* – Nancy Foy's law says that 'the effectiveness of a network is inversely proportional to its formality'; it needs a spider, not a chairperson, and a telephone; all successful organizations have them.

The more *differences* you have to take account of in your structure, in other words, the more you will need to find ways of *integrating* the different parts. Diversity creates a pressure for uniformity. There are three main ways of holding an organization together:

- the hierarchy of command;
- rules and procedures; and
- co-ordinating groups.

Most organizations of any size end up by using all three, because the hierarchy of command turns out to be too cumbersome in practice, and rules and procedures too rigid. But there is this clear sequence to the way any organization develops its integrating devices.

The hierarchy of command

To start with, any problem gets referred up to the lowest cross-over point in the hierarchy, the point where one person effectively oversees the two or more parts of the organization involved in the problem. In a tiny organization one person can do this easily, in effect having meetings in his or her head, which is a good description of a Zeus organization. As things get bigger this way of doing things gets more difficult (because Zeus is too busy, not there or out of touch). When the lowest cross-over point is more than two layers above the point in the hierarchy where the problem exists, then it is usually found to be too difficult, too remote and too slow. Tall thin organizations work efficiently only when there is very little diversity. Rapidly growing or changing organizations are *flat* organizations – see Box 7.4.

Flat organizations, however, don't solve the problems of integration; they magnify them. Most people can integrate only six or seven overlapping areas of work. Give someone ten or twelve subordinates and those subordinates will, inevitably, have to be left largely to their own devices, which is fine as long as they are responsible people whom you can trust and as long as there are other mechanisms for integration and co-ordination when they need it. Twelve people, after all, means nearly eighty potential relationships, all of them different, within that one group.

Box 7.4 Tall or flat?

- The bigger the organization the more levels you need, *unless* you increase the spans of control.
- Tall structures and narrow spans restrict responsibility. The Fulton Committee identified departments in the British Civil Service with nine levels and spans of control of two or three.
- Most organizations need only five levels to do the work; the biggest may need seven. Extra levels are often more to do with power and empire-building than efficiency.
- No manager should supervise the work of more than six subordinates whose work interlocks (said Urwick in 1956).
- Sears Roebuck deliberately increased the span of control of store managers so that they would be forced to delegate, which was effective if the work did not interlock.
- One Japanese bank has over 100 managers reporting to an area manager, but their work does not overlap.

Rules and procedures

Rules and procedures are one way out of the dilemma. Nobody likes rules, but procedures are more acceptable. If there are understood ways of doing things, if it is generally agreed that this paper has to be notified, this form filled in, this committee consulted, if limits of discretion are clearly known and other people's responsibilities respected, then integration is or should be more or less automatic. No one should be too resistant to rules and procedures, because they are, or should be, the neutral alternative to integration from above. Computers, in theory, make the procedures more relevant and neutral, because more impersonal and instantaneous.

Rules and procedures are the hallmark of the Apollo role culture; and as we saw, that culture works well and effectively in stable and routine situations. In other words, when the differences don't differ over time you can have a very flat organization, co-ordinated by procedures, monitored through computers. That is what happens in the Japanese bank mentioned in Box 7.4.

Most voluntary organizations do not inhabit such a world and so find that their procedures are not designed to cope with the sort of problems they encounter. But they should always take care to see that it isn't just their natural Dionysian dislike of rules and regulations which stops them codifying more of what they do. Dionysians do not always realize that regulations actually give you freedom (within the regulations). A well-defined do'nut is permission to exercise discretion within the do'nut. No do'nut and your every move is potentially subject to another's will.

Co-ordinating groups

Most organizations of any size are therefore driven in the end to the third of the devices: co-ordinating groups. The simplest example of such a group is the work group itself. A complete job shop, as previously described, contains within itself all the functions and the skills which need to be co-ordinated; seen as an 'autonomous group', it is actually a self-integrating device. Organizations should look out for the possibility of vesting more groups with the power and the resources to control their own destiny. Not only is it more motivating but it requires less of the time and attention of those higher up.

Why are we often so reluctant to give groups full control over the means to ensure their own objectives? Why are we often so reluctant to group people together in such a way that all the necessary skills belong to one group? Do we not trust them or do we not want to give away some of the power that comes from dividing them up and supervising them separately?

Not all work, however, can be regrouped so that it can be done by just one set of people. The functions, products, clients and regions need to be integrated lest they pull each other apart. In fact, each is integrating the others in its own way. The 'schools' department is making sure that the functions, the products and the regions are aware of its requirements, and the same goes for the other divisions of diversity. But, once again, if everyone is looking to their part of the ship, who is minding the bridge? The most common answer is committees. Committees are the places where compromises are carved out, information is exchanged, bargains are struck and plans agreed. Apollonian by nature, inhibiting and time-consuming and frustrating, they are the necessary bridges in a complex organization. But there is one caveat: committees are there to regulate diversity. Without the diversity, they are an unnecessary nuisance.

One would expect voluntary organizations to prefer flat structures, with few layers and the minimum of hierarchy. Yet voluntary organizations have also got their fair share of differences and diversity of effort. In their need to hold things together they can fall back on hierarchy as a simpler device than procedures and co-ordinating groups. In so doing they are untrue to themselves, probably because they are not aware of the alternatives. To understand is, as ever, to put choice in place of chance.

The shape of the organization

Organizations have always wanted to be big enough to cope with a range of activities (because that makes them more effective and gives them more clout) but also to be small enough to have a common identity (and because small is at least easier to run if not more beautiful). In recent years they have experimented with two ways of doing this, both of which radically affect the shape of the total organization.

The two experiments are:

- the federal organization; and
- the shamrock organization.

Box 7.5 The unintended Zeus

The Rights for Women group which had started with a few angry women at the edge of a northern town was blossoming. They now had two official candidates standing for local elections, a theatre group, an educational project for secondary schools, a media officer, a shop, an industrial relations study group and their own restaurant. They were busy, so busy in fact that they had no time for meetings or for discussing priorities and procedures. They left all that to Jane, and Jane, as she said, had meetings with herself.

It all went like a bomb; and then the bomb exploded. The restaurant had got into debt, which Jane dealt with by a loan from the theatre group, which they weren't too happy about when they found out. The shop refused to stock the materials and books needed for the schools project on the grounds that there was too little margin, and Jane was forced to overrule them. The media officer resigned, and Jane took her place for a while, much to the disgust of the head of the industrial relations study group, who had longed for that role. One evening in the restaurant the disaffected ones found themselves together. Jane, they agreed, had become a dictator, behaving in the way men had behaved down the ages. Jane, meanwhile, was on the verge of collapse; holding the organization together was proving to be beyond her. There had to be a better way.

There is, but it involves budgets, plans and committees, and quite a lot of trust. Diversity demands bridges.

Both raise new questions. Both are here to stay. Both need to be taken seriously by the larger voluntary organization, because they offer a way out of the dilemma of the pyramid – how do you grow bigger without growing taller, with more and more layers of command, more bureaucracy, more of the chores of organizing and proportionately less of the fun?

The federal organization

Federalism is an unfamiliar concept to the British, who remain at heart a monarchical, centralist society. Federalism was reserved for departing colonies and defeated enemies, and the fact that it seems to have served them well was hardly noticed. Any hint of federalism in national affairs is pushed aside, Scotland and Northern Ireland being seen as exceptions not examples.

And so it has been until recently with Britain's organizations. Decentralization has occasionally been flirted with but decentralization is very different from federalism. In decentralized structures the centre is still in command but has delegated a range of tasks to the periphery. In federalist constitutions the centre is the residuary body, doing the things which the parts cannot or do not want to do – delegation the other way round. Federal organizations are *reverse-thrust* organizations, in that the energy and initiative come from the parts not from the centre. The centre does not command or direct in these organizations, it co-ordinates, facilitates and enables.

These organizations are *tight–loose* organizations. They get the reverse thrust by holding loosely on to a lot of things (often the 'hows' of life, 'how' you manage the outfit, 'how' you recruit, staff and pay it, 'how' you organize the work) but holding tight to a few, often including new money (i.e. capital expenditure or new funding) and new people (i.e. key appointments). One of the key strategic decisions for organizations today is the decision on what to hold tight and what to let loose, and it is never quite the same for any two organizations.

Federal organizations need to delegate responsibility in order to keep their flexibility. But they need to set limits to that delegated responsibility lest they lose all control and with it any possibility of co-ordination and of the benefits of size. The definition of the group do'nuts thus becomes crucially important in federal organizations, as does a fundamental belief in subsidiarity.

Box 7.6 Low-profile centre

Switzerland is, in most people's eyes, an example of an effective, well-run country, a country moreover which manages to do well without a steel industry, a car industry or indeed most of the mandatory accessories of the well-dressed industrial nation apart from a rather low-profile but well-run airline.

How does it do it? Federalism is generally accepted as being one of the keys to its success, with power over most matters residing in the cantons or with the individual citizen through referendums. Such an effective federalism should be a model to others, and the man or woman in charge of it should be a name to admire and to emulate. Who, then, is the President of Switzerland?

The fact that no one ever knows, partly because the job rotates, is an outward and visible sign of a largely invisible centre. Would the centres of an organization be content to be so low-profile?

Federalism *ought* to be welcomed by the voluntary world because it can reflect the different priorities of different groups whilst flying the same flag over all of them. The North and the South can, under federalism, agree to be different in degree but not in kind. The campaigners in the movement can run a different culture from their service-providing brothers and sisters but agree that they are united in a common cause. But for *ought* to become *does*, the centres of these organizations have to understand the principles of federalism; be willing to see things done in different ways in different bits; control by results not by procedures; be happy while not always knowing what is going on in other places; be able only to suggest, influence and encourage, not command or tell.

The shamrock organization

The shamrock is a three-petalled leaf, symbolizing for St Patrick and the Irish the mystery of the Trinity, three persons in one God. Applied to organizations its meaning is more mundane: three types of work-force in one organization.

It used to be that organizations had, and wanted to have, only one type of worker: full-time employees, some of whom were managers, others staff experts, others ordinary workers. As the pay of ordinary workers increased, organizations began to understand that this was an expensive way of doing things. As a first response to increasing labour and managerial costs they cut down on the number of employees, but there is a limit to how far you can go with manpower cuts and still keep the organization going. It was then that they realized that you don't need all the people around for all of the time in order to run the organization.

Organizations now increasingly have three categories of people working for and with them. Most importantly there is the *professional core*, the managers, supervisors, technical professional people, the skilled workers without whom the organization would not function and who between them hold what might be called the organizational knowledge required to do the key jobs. Such people are precious to the organization. It is they who have the long-term contracts, plus whatever perks and benefits are going, plus the real power. In return the organization wants their commitment, their flexibility and their willingness to go anywhere, do anything, be available almost any time.

To treat everyone this way would be both unnecessary and expensive. Many skills and services can be bought in more cheaply from outside, more cheaply because you are usually not buying whole jobs but only part of someone's or some group's output, and because the smaller organization or the individuals themselves do not have to carry all the overheads of the larger organization. This, then, is the *contractual fringe* which surrounds more and more organizations these days, made up of individual experts or providers, of small co-operative groups or simply small commercial enterprises selling to the bigger organizations that make up their market-place.

To these two groups, the professional core and the contractual fringe, must today be added a third, the *flexible labour force*, the people who come to work not for a career or for all of their time, but for part of their time, for a decent working environment, for companionship and friends but chiefly for money in exchange for labour. The growth of the service sector and the need to be available to one's customers and clients for more than forty hours a week have meant that organizations have increasingly started to use a part-time work-force to extend the working day and the working week, to cope with peaks and troughs in demand and with the holiday season. It is, after all, cheaper to pay part-timers than to pay regular employees extra to work overtime, assuming they were willing to do it.

So far have these changes in working practices gone that the self-employed on the contractual fringe and the part-timers together now add up to half as many as all the full-time employees. Organizations therefore have to recognize that the shape of their work-force has now changed radically. The point is that each of these groups needs to be handled differently; you cannot assume the same loyalty and commitment, for instance, from the contractual fringe or the flexible labour force as you can from the professional core.

Voluntary organizations have long lived with a slightly different shamrock. For many of them the professional core is made up of paid staff, whilst the volunteers make up the flexible labour force. The contractual fringe is also often a voluntary activity if one thinks of the arrangements for fund-raising, for catering or transport, sometimes for typing or book-keeping, being contracted out for free. But the fact that the cash payments are little or nothing does not affect the fact that those are different categories of workers, with different needs and a different relationship with the organization than the full-time staff.

Box 7.7 Professionals and/or volunteers?

Some voluntary organizations, including the Marriage Guidance Council, the Samaritans, the mountain rescue teams and the Royal National Lifeboat Institution, have a largely volunteer professional core. In many ways this is the purest essence of volunteering, the giving of one's professional skills for free. But it runs up against the organizational requirements of the professional core, namely that they be fully committed, flexible and available. Few people can afford to give their professional skills to a volunteer body on the full-time and full-commitment basis required of the professional core.

For the organization the problem then arises of whether volunteer professionals are not more truly to be regarded as individuals or groups on the contractual fringe, or whether, if they are to be the professional core, they should not then be paid, thus distorting the volunteer principle. In their confusion over this issue organizations can get very heated. They should not need to, as long as they realize that all organizations have more than one classification of worker and that they should be arguing about which part of the shamrock they belong to, not whether they are paid or unpaid.

The flexible labour force, for instance, does not expect the work to be intrinsically rewarding or motivating. But they do expect to be treated fairly, not like slaves, to be given proper notice of when they are needed and to have some control over their work with a reasonable variety (see earlier in this chapter). And they expect people to remember that they all have another life outside the organization.

The contractual fringe needs to know what has to be done, by when, in what quantities and at what standard. They then like to be left alone to get on with it, not to be treated as if they were like the rest of the employees. They have, in other words, to be managed by results not procedures. It is not always easy for those in the centre to realize the need or to remember to treat these categories differently. It is all too easy, for instance, to assume that the part-time helper is as committed as you are, when they may, in truth, be doing it more to break the monotony in their own lives, or for social interaction, than because of commitment to the cause.

8

The Systems of Organizations

The structure may be the skeleton of the organization and the people its flesh and blood, but it is the systems which are its nerves. Without a nervous system in proper order a body will be just that, a body, not an effective human being. Similarly, organizations of any size need to have their proper nervous systems which communicate signals and alert the centre to things that go wrong, which help it to think ahead and allow the different parts of the body to contribute to its general well-being.

In more mundane terms, organizations need

- communications systems;
- number systems; and
- participation systems.

In tiny organizations these things can be done informally, the sums done on the back of an envelope, the necessary meetings carried out in a car on the way to a conference or a client. As the organization grows, however, the sums and the chat can no longer be left to chance, they have to be designed, formalized and monitored, or the organization will remain an anarchic collection of individual activities, small and usually ineffective. A gut reaction against the systems and procedures of Apollo is understandable but it can also be a self-imposed sentence to continuing marginality.

Proper systems are pathways not prisons, telephone

wires not fences. They are the discipline which gives purpose to liberty, which allows one to be free yet part of a bigger whole. They cannot be left to chance because the principles on which they are built are not instinctively obvious. A better understanding of these principles should make it easier to choose between the possibilities.

Communications systems

Communications do not just happen, they have to be worked at. There are few organizations which do not complain of poor communications, few people who don't feel that others know more about what is going on than they do, few of us who don't secretly hug information to ourselves on occasion. Most of us, nevertheless, actually think of ourselves as good communicators, forgetting that for a communication to exist it has to be received as well as sent.

It is salutary to note the following discoveries about communications 'fall-out':

- A study of the production department of a British firm found that a department manager recorded himself, over a period, as having given 165 instructions or decisions. His deputies recorded receiving instructions on only 84 of those occasions, a fall-out of nearly 50 per cent.
- A study at Columbia University discovered that the retention of content matter at the end of a lecture was only 50 per cent – a figure that dropped to 25 per cent after two weeks.
- A study of information dissemination in 100 United States firms found that, of information disseminated by the president, the first level down recalled receiving only 63 per cent, the third level only 40 per cent and the fifth level only 20 per cent.

If only half of what you say is heard or remembered, can you be sure which half it is?

Apart from selective fall-out there are other problems:

- *Distortion by the sender* – in one research study, individuals with career ambitions were found to be systematically withholding information threatening to their positions. Information protection is a common factor in organizational power games.
- *Lack of trust* – a study of scientists demonstrated that when an individual does not fully trust a recipient he or she tends to conceal his or her own views and opinions. In another study only 10 per cent of sixty-seven executives told the news of an incident to more than one other person.
- *Distortion by the receiver* – 'who you are sounds so loudly in my ears that I cannot hear what you say,' commented Dr Johnson. We filter what we hear through our perception of the sender. We can also tone down or tune out unwelcome information by casting doubt on its source. 'Who need listen to a man like that?' we say, or 'She would say that, wouldn't she?'
- *Distance* – one study showed that a flight of three steps between two groups cut communications by 30 per cent. The more immediate drowns out the more distant, just as telephones are too often allowed to interrupt conversations. It is said that when Maynard Keynes met with President Roosevelt there were so many telephone interruptions that he excused himself, went outside and rang in, explaining to a surprised President that 'This seems to be the only way to communicate with you.'
- *Lack of clarity* – what is clear and concise to you may be unintelligible to others. My observation may be jargon to you, my revealing metaphor gobbledegook. Most people write and speak in very loose constructions, and much of what is written is actually never read, by anyone.

Considering these facts, which are familiar to all of us, it is remarkable that any communication takes place at all in organizations. Equally remarkable is the feeling we all have that in some mysterious way these problems do not affect our own communications. Every lecturer and every speech-writer still assumes that every word will be both heard and remembered; every chairperson labours over their opening remarks in the confident expectation that they will all be absorbed and acted upon. Every memorandum is thought by its author to be a definitive piece of communication. Indeed, every author assumes that every word of his or her book will be read, in spite of abundant evidence to the contrary.

Box 8.1 The communication gap

In a study of power-plants by Floyd Mann:

- 35 per cent of the workers say their foreman understands their problems;
- *but* 95 per cent of the foremen say they understand the problems of the workers.

- Fifty-one per cent of these foremen say that their general foreman understands *their* problems;
- *but* 90 per cent of the general foremen say that they understand their foremen's problems.

- Sixty-three per cent of these general foremen say that top staff understand *their* problems;
- *but* 100 per cent of the top staff say that they do.

See *Understanding Organizations*, p. 358.

Busy people tend to take communications for granted. They should not. The following rules of thumb should help:

- Use more than one medium and more than one net. In one study it was found that 60 per cent of the work-force got their information from reading things and 40 per cent from talking to people. Informal channels can sensitize the receiver to formal information. If you know in advance whom you are going to meet at a party you will remember the formal introductions much better.

The 'Budget day' principle, or keeping big news secret, is almost always a bad tactic. Leaks often take the pain out of information and prepare the ear of the recipient.

- Encourage two-way communication. Passive listeners are poor listeners. Wherever possible encourage questions, discussions, argument and participation. Every study shows that while this sort of communication takes much longer it is also much more effective. The quick briefing is quickly forgotten or disowned.
- Avoid links in the chain. The studies show that there is an inevitable filtering effect as communications go through layers. Whenever possible do it directly. The best way to improve communications is not to polish the communication more avidly but to remove as many as possible of the distorting factors and the blocks.

Anyone who understands the fragile nature of communications within organizations will never again leave them to chance. But neither will they be so naïve as to think that a newsletter or another circular will be enough to solve the problem. Successful leaders, it has been observed, are forever talking, to everyone.

Number systems

All organizations need numbers of one sort or another. Few people like numbers. Therein lies the dilemma. No organization can function properly unless it has some way of knowing whether it is moving in the direction it wants to move and how fast and far it is moving. That sounds an obvious enough statement until you try testing it out. Ask a staff member in an organization, any organization, how successful they were last year and wait for them to pause, scratch their head and say, 'Well, it depends . . .'

This is because most organizations have several different levels of success. At one level most organizations are concerned to survive financially. If therefore they can pay their bills or meet all their financial obligations they could say that they have been successful at that level. But that said, they have not done, for there is more. There are some who envy the business corporations, believing that life is simpler for them because the financial criteria are all there is. They are wrong. It is only the sterile corporation that sees profit as the goal rather than a means to greater goals. The great businesses talk of being the best in their field, or the biggest, of growth or of longevity through a succession of products. Indeed, critics have argued that the emphasis by British business on short-term profits has been partly responsible for its long-term relative decline.

The first requirement for any organization, then, is to be clear about its different levels of success and to know how to measure them, what the critical numbers are. That is not easy. Fine words, great phrases and high aspirations do not automatically turn into measurable goals, but it saves a lot of trouble and conflict to *assume* that they do. Liam Welsh once brilliantly and ironically listed twenty-eight ways to ruin a voluntary organization (in *Management Development Unit Bulletin*, September 1983), of which twelve were to do with muddled or untackled definitions of purpose, of what success would mean. For instance, for surefire failure he cynically advised:

- Always view your organization as an end in itself rather than the means.
- Pay particular attention to ensuring that your organization's actions contradict its written and spoken statements (claim to be developing the community's management expertise when the community has irrefutable evidence that you would be hard put to run a bath on a good day).
- Make goals open-ended. Do not develop or argue steps by means of which the goals can be achieved. That way nobody can begin to work on them.
- Make sure that as few people as possible know what is going on in the organization.
- Prevent your organization establishing what it is good

at doing. Better still, get staff to concentrate their attention on trying to improve what they are already bad at doing.

Would that Liam Welsh's irony had less basis in reality.

Box 8.2 The fork-tongued organization

- 'We stand for the relief of poverty in all its forms,' said the chairperson in that grandiloquent voice, perfected over time in their Lordships' House.
- 'If we can get this government to understand that one in five of the people in this country are in poverty, we shall have made a breakthrough' – a staff member.
- 'We need at least another one thousand covenanted members or we shall have to close down' – the accountant.
- 'The journal is our principal product. I measure our impact by its circulation, which I'm pleased to say is growing' – the editor.
- 'I tried them. They said there was nothing they could do to help' – a single parent on supplementary benefit.

Who is describing the goals of the organization – all or none?

Most organizations have or should have:

- A cause, a vision or an overriding purpose, one which is long on rhetoric and short on numbers. That is fine, since its purpose is to inspire rather than to direct activity. But if anything is to happen, the cause must be supported by:
- A set of specific tasks or areas of specific activity to be tackled in support of that cause.
- And a set of measures which will indicate what success means in each task.

That third item is the number system. It is merely a piece of organizational clutter if it is unconnected to the other two, while the other two without it are but empty words.

Remember, too, that numbers matter more than words; the hard overrides the soft. Schools, for instance, may proclaim that they are more concerned for the overall development of the individual than with any scores in examinations but as long as they have numbers for the second and only words for the first it will be examinations which come to determine success in the eyes of teachers, parents and children (a glance at any school prospectus will show up this dichotomy).

Numbers matter. That truth needs to be engraved in the mind of anyone trying to run an organization. They had therefore better be the right numbers in the right place at the right time, or the 'E' factors in the organization will get distorted or become random. That said, there is a set of questions that the designer of the number system needs to consider:

- Before or after the event? Some organizations design their systems so that no one can make a serious mistake. All decisions of any significance, and the numbers on which they are based, have to be advised to a higher authority before any action is permitted. In other organizations the numbers are not known until after the action has happened. Many organizations have both systems. It is a crucial choice and should not be left to chance. After-the-event numbers allow more discretion to the individual or the group but make mistakes more possible. After-the-event numbers are best suited to situations where the work can be divided up into relatively *independent* activities, so that one person's mistake does not affect anyone else. In *sequential* or integrated operations (as in a factory or a chemical plant), where one person's mistake can affect a whole sequence of activity, the cost of a mistake may be too high, and therefore before-the-event numbers will be needed – that is, more plans and schedules, more of an Apollo role culture, in fact.
- Is success more than not failing? Many number systems

only highlight failure, or below-target achievement. Success then becomes not failing, satisfying, dealing with only the core of the do'nut. Good number systems distinguish between 'necessary' and 'sufficient' numbers. A 'necessary' level of achievement is not usually 'sufficient' to ensure success.

- Do the numbers fit the people? The numbers must have some fairly direct relationship to individual or group effort if they are going to mean anything. The numbers that go into a typical annual report may be appropriate for the outside world and for its representatives on the management committee but they are often too total and too late to have much meaning for the individual staff member. Good production systems find a way of telling each group how its performance has stood up against targets each *day* or each *week*.
- What sort of numbers are they? The numbers do not have to be financial ones; indeed, the language of money is seldom the language used in practice by most of the work groups in any organization. They will talk instead of things produced, things used, people served or clients dealt with, hours worked or people involved. Beware, however, lest the numbers distort activity in an unintended direction, like the hospital which decided that patient turn-round time was the criterion of success for each ward, only to find that wards became reluctant to admit long-stay patients no matter how ill they were. Different parts of the organization will certainly want different sorts of numbers. The management committee will not normally want to see the detailed numbers which are needed by the task groups and should not be burdened by them.
- What numbers do the numbers relate to? Numbers by themselves are nearly always meaningless. To say that you have overspent by £20,000 in the year may be trivial if you are the National Trust but catastrophic for a young community project. All numbers, it is probably true to say, need to be expressed as a percentage of

some other number. Sometimes that number will be the equivalent figure last year, sometimes it will be the budgeted figure for this year, sometimes it will be a totally different number altogether but then compared with past or future equivalents. The choice of *ratio* (is it clients per staff member, clients per £100,000 p.a., income as a percentage of capital or costs per member?) is a crucial decision that needs careful thought at the top of the organization, because numbers always affect effort.

- How are the target numbers arrived at? In Chapter 2 we saw that the very act of setting your own targets and goals has an energizing effect. One would therefore expect organizations to encourage people to set their own numbers, having arrived at an agreed definition of success. Unfortunately it is not as simple as that, because everyone is well aware that the numbers can be used for other purposes. If, for instance, the numbers are also going to be used to evaluate the performance of the individual, instinct would suggest that the individual would want, in the interests of safety, to keep them low. Yet if the numbers were going also to be used as the basis for allocating more resources, office space or staff, then the temptation might be to boost them. This is the trouble with budgets – see Box 8.3 – they cannot simultaneously be used as a plan, a target and a basis for reward. There are no easy answers. One compromise is to involve the individuals in the definition of success and failure and to add the numbers later, based on some extrapolation of historical performance.

- What lies behind the numbers? Numbers are crucial, rather as a speedometer and a petrol-gauge are crucial to any sensible motorist; but they are never the whole story. They are indicators and, like the petrol-gauge, they can at times be faulty indicators. One should *never* assume that they tell the whole truth; one should *always* look for the explanation behind the unexpected. To do any less is to ignore the individual or the group of individuals who made those numbers happen; it is to turn the organization into a numbers game with the implicit message that people and causes don't matter; it is to run the risk that any future numbers would be faulty without you knowing which. *The number system must always be the servant not the master*, the indicator not the engine.

Box 8.3 The trouble with budgets

There has always been a problem with budgets. Back in the 1950s Argyris, investigating budgets in some large US companies, found that:

- The budget staff regarded themselves as watchdogs for top management.
- The accountants saw budgets as challenges to the line staff.
- The line staff thought they were a basis for judging them and were unfair because they were inflexible.
- The foremen resented the pressure on them to meet budgets, feeling that it implied they were lazy or incompetent.
- The top management felt that budgets should be realistic, but the financial people wanted them as optimistic as possible.
- The middle management wanted them as easy as possible.

Things have not changed much in the last thirty years. Budgets still cause problems basically because the same set of figures cannot be used:

- as the basis for a plan;
- as operational data to liaise with other groups;
- as a stimulant to higher performance;
- as a way of evaluating performance.

- When does a computer help? Computers are quick. They can turn raw data into the ratios and percentages you need in seconds. They can plot figures in graphs, turn them into account statements, break them up and down any which way. The danger, of course, is that they build a high pyramid of analysis on a rather flimsy base and that those who see the tip of the pyramid no longer know what lies behind the numbers. One rule of thumb could be to respect the *speed* of the computer but to distrust its *analysis* unless you could, if need be, do it yourself with pencil, paper and maybe a calculator. Computers are most reliable when they are dealing with *absolute* numbers, as in the physical sciences, in robots, process plants and aeroplanes. They are less to be trusted when dealing with the *relative* numbers which are what organizations have to deal in, numbers which are indicators only, not necessarily facts.

People are more important than numbers. That feeling runs through the voluntary world and is an attractive part of its culture. To reverse it would be wrong, but to take it as permission to ignore the numbers would be foolish. To do that is, ironically, to raise to a false prominence those numbers which you have to have, usually the financial ones, but which may not be the crucial ones. Numbers beat words every time. So it is important that the key words end up with numbers attached to them. The number system cannot be left to chance, it is too important for that. Neglect it and it will distort the organizational effort.

Participation systems

Nowhere in the context of the structures of organizations (Chapter 7) did we discuss management committees, or the rights of members. There was no mention of elections, annual general meetings, representatives or constitutions; yet these are part of the air of voluntary organizations, and at times they seem to be the whole atmosphere. They were not discussed under structure because they are not part of the delivery system of the organization; they do not explain how the work gets done or who does it. What they are to do with is the accountability system, the whys and whats of the organization and the rights of its members and its constituency to be involved in the policy-making process and in the purpose-moulding of the organization.

To call the democracy that is inherent in voluntary organizations a system is, perhaps, to belittle it. That is not the intention. The point of including it in this chapter is to remind organizations that it is something to be thought about systematically and to be designed into organizations rather than taken for granted or left to chance and history; for democracy comes in many guises, and participation has many forms. There is a choice. The main alternatives are:

- Direct democracy – the pure collective or autonomous group.
- Representative democracy – with an elected council of members.
- Stakeholder democracy – a management committee and an executive team.

The choice of democratic form is often decided by circumstances. A small membership organization will often want direct democracy with its appealing rejection of hierarchy, outside control and differentiation of roles and tasks. But success makes things more difficult for such collectives. The transaction costs of running the place get out of proportion, roles and tasks are clearly no longer equal, some people are obviously more equal than others – see Box 8.4.

Successful collectives tend therefore to become representative democracies. They elect some of themselves to positions of influence and control, although retaining major decisions, including all constitutional issues, for direct democracy at an annual general meeting or via occasional referendums.

It is when the membership organization becomes a service organization that the rights of the other stakeholders have to be thought of, the clients, the funding agencies, the community at large. At this stage there is pressure to bring representatives of those groups into the governing process. So, little by little, the representative democracy gives way to stakeholder democracy, with a council or management committee made up of representatives of *all* the stakeholder groups, including the membership.

Box 8.4 The collective dream

The non-hierarchical, self-organizing, self-managing group is the dream of many, not only in the voluntary sector. It is built on a belief in the capacity of the individual, every individual, on a repudiation of levels and of one set above another, and on a desire that those who strive collectively should own the aim of their striving.

There are problems, however:

- Who arranges tasks, decides priorities, gives responsibility? A system of meetings and of decision-rules has to be arranged, together with training in the ways of groups, the setting of priorities, the processes of accountability and sharing information.
- Who carries the ultimate responsibility? Some form of legal trust or limited liability is usually necessary for money to be collected. Who should be the trustees? What is their relationship to the members or to the other members? Can all members be trustees?
- Does everyone belong to the collective or is there an inner and an outer group, *à la* shamrock, with some duties which cannot be shared or rotated, such as keeping the books, secretary, special consultant, viewed as contract labour?
- Does everyone get paid the same if everyone is paid at all? If so, how do you deal with new arrivals who lack the experience and skill of the older members?

Dreams without systems (and hard decisions) can become nightmares as the transaction costs of a group exceed its output.

Each of these forms of democracy is appropriate in its

proper circumstances. Each will work provided that some principles of democracy are remembered and respected. These are that:

- Participation in policy-making needs to be separated from participation in executive decision-making.
- Consultation, consent and consensus are all forms of participation but different.

'The people should decide *what* should be done and then give it to others to do.' Parliament is there to pass laws, educate the nation and choose the executive – see Box 8.5. It is appropriate for the members of an organization either directly or through their chosen representatives to debate policy. It is when they want to debate and agree every executive action that the transaction costs begin to exceed the output.

What is policy and what is execution is, unfortunately, never clear. In one organization a change in retirement age from 65 to 55 was seen as an executive decision, whilst in another the setting of mileage allowances was thought to be worth one hour of discussion in the policy-making body. Some executive decisions are clearly landmark decisions and rank as policy. Some policies are more like executive rules than guide-paths to the future. One of the key choices that people at the centre of an organization have to make is whether something is a policy matter or an executive decision. To take the easy way out and make every executive act a policy matter is to bog down the organization in trivia and often to neglect to spend enough time on the bigger and longer-term issues of true policy.

Collectives have to learn to design do'nuts, to allocate tasks and responsibilities and to let people get on with them. Membership organizations have to be disciplined enough not to crowd agendas with personal hobby-horses, pushing their point of view up through branch and region to national level like some appeal court procedure. Chairpersons of management committees need to guard the agenda lest their meetings become just a review of other people's decisions referred upwards for approval. Management committees and executive committees are indeed most inappropriately named, for managing and executing are precisely what they should *not* be doing.

Box 8.5 The purposes of Parliament – by Walter Bagehot

Bagehot outlined five purposes for Parliament in his book, *The English Constitution*:

- The House of Commons is a choosing body; it approves the choice of premier and can dismiss him or her. 'They guide him and he leads them. He is to them what they are to the nation. He only goes where he believes they will go after him. But he has to take the lead.'
- The House of Commons has an expressive function. 'It is its office to express the mind of the English people on all matters which come before it.'
- 'The third function of Parliament is what I call . . . the teaching function. A great and open council of considerable men cannot be placed in the middle of a society without altering that society . . . It ought to teach the nation what it does not know.'
- 'The House of Commons has an informing function – to lay before the nation the grievances and complaints of particular interests.'
- 'Lastly, there is the function of legislation, of which of course it would be preposterous to deny the importance.'

Perhaps more management committees should study Walter Bagehot.

Consent and consensus are not the same thing, nor is consultation:

- *Consultation* means that the leader listens, pays heed but then decides. Obviously any leader who, having consulted, ignores the advice and the preferences is living dangerously. But in theory this is possible in extreme situations where the leader rates his or her opinion or knowledge as of overriding importance.

- *Consent* means that the group has a power of veto on any decision, but it is the leader's, or someone's, job to put the decision to the group. Consent cannot operate in a vacuum.
- *Consensus* means that the group has to go beyond not vetoing something but has positively to agree it. Apathy, indifference or just equanimity is not enough. Consensus is the toughest form of participation.

Box 8.6 Decisions in federations

Contradictions are a necessary part of the decision-making process in federal organizations. What seems right from one perspective may seem crazy from another. Federal organizations have to live with contradictions and make a place for them in their decision-making structures. This point is made by Karin Jonnergard and Associates in their book on *Co-operative Decision-Making (Beskit i Kooperative?)* (Stockholm, Raben & Sjogren, 1984).

They suggest that:

- The decision-makers need to encourage new formulations of problems and contradictions, not iron them out in the search for a quick consensus.
- Specific 'arenas' should be created for the different parties to meet to share their perceptions.
- Preparatory documents should be drawn up to lay out the perspectives, so that personalities do not dominate and information is shared as widely as possible.
- Only after a full discussion and acceptance of the differences and contradictions should the organization try to reach a decision. This will, paradoxically perhaps, be easier after everyone has had a chance to express their viewpoint and hear the others.

It takes time and costs money but it is worth it.

It is too often assumed that democracy and participation mean *consensus*. Because consensus is difficult to achieve, particularly in federal organizations – see Box 8.6 – a frustrated leadership will often move towards autocracy or government by cabal (Zeus club culture). In practice, *consent* is a sensible middle way. It avoids the sometimes horrendous transaction costs and compromises of consensus without giving unbridled power to the leader, particularly if the guiding policies have already been established.

There is one more fundamental principle of democracy – that of *limited tenure*. Real power is given to someone for only a fixed period of time. Prime ministers and presidents have to stand for re-election, lest they become dictators, abuse their power or start to take the wrong decisions. Give someone effective tenure and you soon make sure that the position has no real power, is hedged around with restrictions and the rights of others. Who need listen to bishops, professors or even the Queen, people in our society with tenure but no power, only influence?

Paradoxically it follows that democracies often work best with strong leaders. The people feel safe because they can get rid of their leader if they disapprove. The leader has power and the support of the people who elected him or her; therefore he or she can afford to rule by consent, confident that most of the time consent will be forthcoming. The organization is therefore run according to the will of the people but run without too many of those transaction costs of meetings, papers and conferences.

The voluntary world does well to remember the principle of limited tenure. Without it, it is hard to trust one's leader. Without it, democracy spills over from policy to execution; without it, consent is not enough, consensus it has to be, in small things as well as big. Leaders should trust their people, but people need to trust their leaders too lest the whole world becomes an endless meeting or a prolonged election campaign. That was never the democratic intention.

9

The Chances of Change

'Things need to change.' 'I hate change.' These two statements, often made by the same person, sum up the paradox
of change. While we can all see the need for improvements
in society, in where we work, in the home, we also dislike
the dislocations and disruptions which change can bring,
particularly if the change is not of our devising and not
under our control.

The splendid plea, heard in a debate in the General Synod
of the Church of England, 'Why cannot the status quo be
the way forward in this matter?' has to be the secret prayer
of many in the comfortable middle structures of life and
organizations. The young, the poor and the ambitious sense
few costs in change in comparison with the possible gains,
but they often have little power to create change. Those
who have the power tend to put the equation the other way
round, seeing the downside risks all too clearly and the
quirkiness of any possible benefit.

Small wonder, then, that most organizations change
only when they are very frightened, when the costs of
no change vastly exceed the risks, which is too often too
late, and even then new people usually have to be brought
in to make the change. Small wonder also that many
organizations can end up like the poor boiling frog – see
Box 9.1 – preferring to turn a deaf ear to the new noises
in their environment.

Box 9.1 The boiling frog

It is said that a frog dropped into boiling water will leap out again at once untouched, but if the same frog is put into cold water and if the temperature be raised ever so slowly, it will not react or move and will eventually, if left there, allow itself to be boiled alive.

Slow changes in the environment can inoculate us all.

Put it another way, however, and few would deny that growth and development are as important to an organization as they are to an individual or to a society. Everyone tends to favour development where few favour change, and we conveniently forget that the one implies the other.

Yet development is a matter not of luck but of discipline, a discipline which can be learned. To run a developing organization requires an understanding of:

- the blocks to change, and how to deal with them; and
- the levers of change, and how to choose between them.

Only then will there be a chance that the organization not only adapts and survives in a world that is always changing, but more importantly keeps its destiny in its own hands and, more importantly still, is a place where individuals can themselves grow, develop and contribute to a better future.

As an epilogue to this book it is fitting to look at the evolving vision for voluntary organizations in an evolving world; to consider the opportunity that must exist to demonstrate that there is another way to run organizations, one which combines the imperative of effectiveness with the rights and needs of human beings.

The blocks to change

There are three main blocks to change, whether we are thinking of organizations or of our own lives. They are:

- blinkers and filters;

- the predictability imperative; and
- the grip of coalitions.

These each need some explanation.

Blinkers and filters

We see what we expect to see. The Peruvian Indians, it is said, literally did not see the approaching ships of their Spanish invaders, although they were as plain as the proverbial pikestaff on the horizon. Because they had no concept of fleets of ships, they put it down to a freak of the weather or to flawed vision.

The business world is full of tales of how management ignored the obvious. Macy's, the big US department store, for twenty years chose to reject the information that appliance sales were more profitable and growing faster than the ready-made garments which had made the company famous. Only when the business had almost collapsed did a new management do the obvious and turn its stores into appliance shops for the masses. 'Appliances' were not what the older management wanted to sell or, therefore, to know about.

Peter Drucker argues that one way to continue to grow and to develop is to look out for the unexpected, and to accept it when you see it. IBM in the 1970s were convinced that personal computers were expensive, uncoordinated and understocked with memories and programs (they were right) and that as a result would be a temporary phenomenon which IBM need not bother about (they were wrong). What was impressive was their acceptance of the unexpected success of the desktop computer, their massive investment in finding their own response and their success, seven years later, in claiming nearly two-thirds of the market.

As individuals we all like to filter the world through familiar spectacles. We read the same newspaper each day, the same periodicals each month; we watch the same TV programmes, meet with familiar friends and colleagues. Everything is designed to reinforce our view of the world and to screen out discordant information or opinion. It used to be bad manners in polite society to talk about politics, religion or women at the dinner table, because that way lay argument, disagreement and information that might not fit the prevailing world-view. No room for the unexpected there.

How many of us, as individuals, go out of our way to listen to those who might disagree with us? How many go to see the parts of the country, or of the world, which they do not know? How many genuinely follow Karl Popper's recipe for the search for truth and deliberately seek to refute or disprove our pet theories? Is it, then, any wonder that the unexpected and the new can creep quite close to us without our noticing it?

Organizations are often no better. Group-think, as we saw in Chapter 4, is one common way of insulating yourself from the unwanted. Reporting systems which focus on what we did rather than on what we might have done or might do, or on what others do, are another way of anchoring us in our current preparations.

The cure is obvious at one level. Expose yourself to differences; look constantly for the opportunities, for other ways of doing things; listen to outsiders; hearken to the young, who often see things that their elders do not; discipline yourself to think of things the other way round – see Box 9.2; do some lateral thinking; imagine that the organization was not there, would you create it the way it is now?

Such well-intentioned resolutions cannot be left to chance or a rainy day. The average manager, we know, seldom has more than ten minutes alone at a stretch to think. Holidays and weekends are an unreliable substitute for organized 'discordant thinking'. But there is nothing to stop the top group of an organization from deliberately arranging two occasions a year, preferably away from the office and including at least one night away, to think differently, looking at divisional reports in terms of missed opportunities, indulging in some scenario dreaming, commissioning radical reports from younger recruits, inviting presentations from credible outsiders, deliberately envisaging one or two impossible situations. The immediate practical outcome on any one occasion might be small, but it would make upside-down thinking respectable, give the unexpected a chance of being noticed and liberate the creative sides of the people present.

Box 9.2 Thinking the other way round

Copernicus upset everyone by suggesting that the Earth went round the Sun rather than the Sun round the Earth.

Rowland Hill's answer to an increasingly costly and ineffective postal service was to introduce a universal 'penny post', the same price everywhere to everyone. He too upset everyone but he fathered the modern postal system.

Xerox realized that no one would pay nearly $5,000 for a copying machine when carbons were so much cheaper, so they decided to charge 5 cents per copy on machines effectively loaned to the customer. Xerox is now a household word.

A US Midwestern stockbroking firm does not offer its clients the opportunities for great profits or the chance to make a fortune but 'peace of mind' by investing their savings in things like deferred annuities, real-estate trusts and investment trusts. Ignored by its competitors on Wall Street, it is now as big as many of them.

The predictability imperative

'I think that I've thought of everything,' says the reception organizer, with the contingency plans for wet weather, the reserve stocks of drink and the carefully rehearsed timetable for the arrival of the minister. The unexpected is very much the unwanted.

It doesn't just apply to parties. Most people want a large

element of predictability in their lives most of the time. The certainty of the dawn makes the miserable night endurable. Carefree youth is made possible for many by the certainty of a home to go back to if freedom goes wrong. Predictability suddenly removed threatens our sense of self, as in redundancy, divorce or severe illness.

Organizations are worse than individuals. The way to efficiency is via predictability. If you know what is going to happen, you can plan to deal with it. If you can *guarantee* that it will happen, then you can dispose of the organization's resources in the most efficient way. The story of the new hospital that regretted the arrival of the patients because they disturbed its quiet efficiency is only partly apocryphal.

Organizations want the world to be predictable, at least a large part of them do. They therefore seek in all sorts of ways to *impose* predictability on their worlds:

- They plan assiduously, hoping that the plans become self-fulfilling prophecies.
- They form alliances, cartels and monopolies, the better to control the unruly environment they serve.
- They lay down rules and procedures to cover who will do what for whom.
- They put the world outside into categories, with clear instructions for dealing with each category.
- They install before-the-event controls to make sure that no mistakes can be made.
- They follow the prescriptions of Rosabeth Moss Kanter – Box 9.3.

This is all both understandable and admirable. Unfortunately it is not cost-free. To attempt to put so much certainty into life, to follow Apollonian traditions and the role culture, makes experiment, innovation and creativity less likely. Development becomes a struggle, and 'change' an ominous word.

We all, organizations included, need predictability. But

Box 9.3 Ten rules for stifling initiative

Rosabeth Moss Kanter studied what she termed 'segmentalism' (Apollonian) companies in the USA and came up with ten rules for stifling initiative:

- Regard any new idea from below with suspicion — because it is new, and because it is from below.
- Insist that people who need your approval to act first go through several other levels of management to get their signatures.
- Ask departments or individuals to challenge and criticize each other's proposals. (Then you can just pick the survivor.)
- Express your criticisms freely, and withhold your praise. (That keeps people on their toes.) Let them know they can be fired at any time.
- Treat problems as signs of failure, to discourage people from letting you know when something in their area isn't working.
- Control everything carefully, make sure people count anything that can be counted, frequently.
- Make decisions to reorganize and change policies in secret and spring them on people suddenly. (That also keeps people on their toes.)
- Make sure that any request for information is fully justified and that it isn't distributed too freely. (You don't want data to fall into the wrong hands.)
- Assign to lower-level managers responsibility for cutbacks and lay-offs.
- Above all, never forget that you at the top already know everything important about this business.

R. M. Kanter, *The Change Masters: Corporate Entrepreneurs at Work* (Allen & Unwin, 1983).

to avoid it becoming the dominant imperative, organizations can do a range of things:

They can explore more carefully. The natural way to ensure predictability is to carry the present with you into the future, thus making sure that nothing changes. Some people, when travelling, like to move in a cocoon of the familiar, from Hilton to Hilton with their watches set to the time back home. Others, by diligent inquiry and research, can make the place they are going to a familiar land long before they ever get there, thus making the new predictable. (Others, of course, prefer to immerse themselves in the novelty without forethought, but such people are not afflicted by the predictability imperative.)

Organizations can do the same. Careful scanning of the world outside and ahead will make the future a familiar territory and the new less strange by the time it is encountered. Don't expect tomorrow to be like yesterday, expect it to be different, guess at the differences, then the surprises will be less. Do it systematically, once or twice a year, and the unforeseeable will gradually become the predictable.

They can build uncertainty into the predictable. Most plans end up as one set of figures, one line pointing into the future. Everyone knows, privately, that those figures are actually the most likely of a set of possibilities, even just the arithmetic average of a set of guesses, if they are not merely last year's numbers with 10 per cent added for luck. Nevertheless, those figures acquire a reality of their own once they are written down and they become the rail to which we cling on our walk to the future, a spurious predictability.

The better plans do not pretend, they expose the guesses and make explicit the range of possibilities, both good and bad. The predictability is still there, but now there is room for manoeuvre; it is a map rather than a rail.

They can encourage exploring. Research and experience demonstrate that those who have moved around a bit in their youth make the more adaptable adults. An exciting youth (contrary to popular wisdom) makes for an exciting life, provided of course that you come through the early excitement unscathed. It is sensible, when you think about it; a predictable youth must make one more dependent on predictability. Organizations cannot reinvent your youth

but they can encourage a bit of exploring. In an organization, exploring could mean new jobs in new places (the
armed services are strong advocates of this policy); it could
mean the assignment, part-time perhaps, to special projects
or task forces; it could mean building bigger do'nuts for
people with the expectation that they exercise their initiative in the empty space. In cultural terms, it can mean giving
Apollonians a taste of Athena.

Predictability in organizations is necessary. Without predictability and its rules, routines and disciplines, anarchy is
inevitable. But predictability carried over into a way of life
makes the new a problem and 'change' a nasty word. Predictability has to be kept in its place if the organization is
to develop.

The grip of coalitions

Mancur Olsen has a thesis that when nation-states mature
then coalitions emerge within them which are more interested, instinctively, in fighting to protect their share or their
corner than in exploring new directions. They each calculate
that they have more to gain from defending or increasing
their own interest than from any 'fall-out' from a growth in
the whole. These coalitions are naturally interested in the
preservation of the status quo, because any change is likely
to disturb their power and interest base, and probably not
for the better.

Anyone seeking to promote change soon runs into these
coalitions. It is not hard to see the evidence for this thesis
in Britain today, and all mature organizations have their
own sets of coalitions as blocks to change.

Mancur Olsen reaches the depressing conclusion that
only wars and disasters can break up the coalitions and that
these therefore become the necessary precursors of change.
In the world of organizations bankruptcy and take-over are
the equivalent, and there is plenty of evidence that it was
only the looming threat of receivership or enforced merger
that unlocked the stranglehold of particular groups on

many an organization's policies and practices. The recorded sequence of major organizational change is depressingly consistent. It goes:

- *fright*, which leads to:
- *new people*, *new thinking* and *new structures*, which result in:
- *new practices*.

This is only further confirmation of Olsen's argument.

As long as they are growing fast, organizations have little to fear from coalitions. New ones are forming, old ones are changing, and there is at least as much to be gained from an increase in the whole as from self-interest. It is at the stage of maturity that this particular form of organizational arthritis sets in.

Once aware of it, there are things that can be done by organizations to prevent this block arising and to lessen its impact:

They can encourage fluidity. Coalitions should not be allowed to gel. In Chapter 8 the concept of limited tenure was noted as one of the principles of federalism. It could also be one of the prerequisites of a growing organization. People ought not to be encouraged or allowed to acquire the rights of statutory tenants to any part of an organization. In the voluntary world this applies particularly to management and executive committees, which have a preference for the re-election of their existing members, for co-option and for committee nomination for new members. Such ways encourage vested rights, and while there is a lot to be said for retaining wisdom and experience in the organization it need not sit always in the same place. Fixed terms of office should be mandatory for all committees.

They can practise Maoism. Chairman Mao maintained that periodic revolutions were necessary to a nation's vitality. He was not always to practise what he preached, but the lesson is valid, and the reasons clear: revolution keeps coalitions from gelling. Many business organizations restructure themselves every few years (usually, for some reason, effective from 1 April). While that may be in order to reflect a changing pattern of diversity (as suggested in Chapter 8), it may also have the underlying rationale of keeping coalitions temporary.

Federalism, by breaking down the organization into semi-autonomous parts, gives any coalition less power over the whole and also makes any restructuring easier and less dramatic. There is, of course, no need to overdo it, like Mao, or to make revolution an annual ritual. But it is worth remembering that there is method in the seeming madness of constant reorganization.

They can sweeten loyalty. Loyalty used to be something an organization or a country could expect, require and demand. Early forms of appraisal used to ask for marks for loyalty. This is today a bad misreading of the psychological contract, indeed a reversal of it. Today the organization has, if anything, to earn the loyalty of the individual. It is not something which you, the superior, can expect but something which you can hope to elicit.

Loyalty is sweetened by participation. If someone feels a sense of ownership of the goals and policies of the place, to that extent they are more committed to it and therefore more prepared to subordinate their own local interests for the good of the whole.

Loyalty is sweetened by reminders. We need to be reminded to feel proud of the cause we serve. The rituals of armies and cathedrals may not be appropriate devices for a voluntary organization, but all the rituals, ceremonials, uniforms and banners have a purpose: to put the cause and the organization above self when it is life itself that may be at stake. Organizations often starve themselves of ceremony and ritual. Perhaps they are missing something, something which needs to be recreated in an appropriate form.

Coalitions will always exist, but they need not be so permanent nor so self-interested if proper care is taken. Without that care they become powerful preservers of the status quo and blocks to change and development.

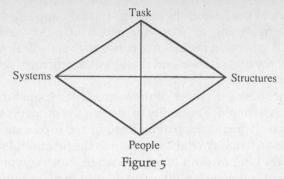

Figure 5

The levers of change

There is a simple diagram, first drawn by Harold Leavitt, which acts as a useful reminder of the levers of change available to any who would act as change-maker in an organization. It looks like Figure 5. It is drawn this way, instead of as a simple list, to make the point that all four levers are interconnected, that they are joined as it were by elastic bands; pull one and the others all change too, although not necessarily to the same degree. This becomes clearer when we look, briefly, at what each involves.

Task

Change the task of a group and, as was noted in Chapter 4, the ways of the group will change. Make a complex task simpler and more structured ways of working immediately become both sensible and acceptable. Change the definition of the task, from making chairs for the handicapped, perhaps, to helping the handicapped to use ordinary chairs, and you obviously change everything the group does, its equipment, its place of work and its way of work, even its people, their training and their supervision. A major change, involving structure, systems of work and the people, will all have stemmed from a redefinition of the task.

Put that on a larger canvas and it relates back to the idea

of cultural confusion, the mix of mutual support, service and campaigning as part and parcel of most voluntary work. A change in the balance between these will affect the style of the organization and therefore its structure, systems and people.

No wonder the power of the visionary or 'transforming' leader is admired. The ability to discern the proper role and focus for an organization or for a group and to communicate that vision in a way which commands the hearts and minds of others is a powerful lever of change. Not everyone can do it, not everyone is allowed to do it or in a position to do it, but it's a good place to start looking if you want to change things.

Box 9.4 The consultant's dilemma

'Come and help us,' the director said. 'Our committee structure needs changing; the whole decision-making structure is bogged down.'

'It's all a question of the director's personality,' they told the consultant when he met the heads of divisions. 'He will insist on getting his way whatever the facts of the situation.'

As the consultant listened to more people it was clear that one-third of the organization believed that they were collecting money for the relief of poverty in the developing world, one-third saw themselves as a developing agency, offering advice backed by money, while one-third were clear that their main job was to educate the people of Britain about the problems of the Third World. The director and one or two others had another agenda again, the reform of oppression and maladministration so that poverty and injustice could be eliminated at source.

No wonder decisions were difficult, arguments common, committee meetings fraught. When all the tasks were justifed, could they all be done? If not, who should have priority and who should decide? One thing was clear; without agreement on the prime task of the organization no rejigging of committees would do any good.

Structures

Playing with structures can feel like playing God. 'Now, if we merge these two departments and call them Central Administration, that will solve much of our problem.' The trouble is, on its own it won't.

One of the most common practices in organizations might be called 'boxing the problem'. This device involves taking the name of the problem, which might be the co-ordination of the regions, and putting that name in a box as the title of a new role in the belief that the problem is now disposed of. All that has happened, of course, is that the new 'co-ordinator of regions' has inherited the problem. If one were really cynical one would say that the problem had now been sewn into the fabric of the organization, had been perpetuated and blessed by the structure.

Structural adaptations are essential in any organization, to keep coalitions fluid and to recognize changing patterns of diversity, new needs for integration or new fields to explore. By themselves, however, structural solutions don't do a lot. People go on doing much the same thing whatever their title may say, unless their task is also modified, the systems adapted and they themselves trained or equipped in some way for the new job.

Systems

We have already examined (in Chapter 8) the importance of getting the right systems, of communications, numbers and participation. Changing these can be a powerful lever. For instance, changing the key numbers used in regional reports from money to services provided or clients catered for can change priorities dramatically. Obviously, to do this without consideration of the task to be achieved would be senseless (which doesn't stop some organizations doing just that).

Systems, however, can be more grandly conceived if we think of them as agents of change. Box 9.5 gives some of

---

Box 9.5 Social inventions

Inventions need not be confined to 'things'. Some of the most important developments in history have been due to the invention of new ways of doing familiar things, new *systems*, social inventions. Peter Drucker reminds us of a few:

In the nineteenth century the American farm industry was becoming impoverished because the average farmer did not have the cash to pay for the machinery which was now available and which he needed to modernize his farm. Cyrus McCormick, one of the manufacturers, invented instalment buying, and the problem was solved.

Until the sixteenth century schooling was essentially a one-on-one relationship between teacher and pupil and therefore inevitably restricted to a few. Comenius, a Czech teacher, invented the idea of a textbook, and universal schooling became possible.

The hospital, an organizational innovation of the eighteenth century, had as much to do with improving health as all the technological discoveries.

August Borsig is known as the first man to build steam locomotives in Germany. Far more important was his creation of the first factory organization, with the *Meister*, or shop-floor supervisor, and the apprenticeship system which are today the foundation of Germany's industrial strength.

In recent times the idea that a ship was a materials-handling device and not a cargo ship resulted in the dramatic growth of the container industry and the transformation of our ports.

P. Drucker, *Innovation and Entrepreneurship* (Heinemann, 1985).

---

history's more exotic examples, but we can all add a few of our own if we sit down and think of new ways of doing old things – social inventions, we might call them – sometimes so obvious that it is hard to think that all things were not always done that way. For example:

- the hospice movement, as a new way of caring for the dying;

- distance learning (as in the Open University), as a new way of relating students to teacher;
- take-away food, as a new way of eating;
- sponsored runs, as a new way of raising money;
- garden centres, as a new way of selling gardening.

Such social inventions owe little to technology, more to the ability to think of new systems.

People

A tempting way to get instant change is to change the people, particularly the people in charge. 'Change' in this sense means finding new people for existing roles. The assumption is that the new person will bring some missing ingredient to the task.

That can often be true, but it is well to be sure in advance what the missing ingredient is. Progress by trial and error can be excessively costly and painful when the trials and errors are named human beings, and the law of the land as well as the traditions of most organizations are weighted against this kind of experimentation by persons. In practice, the scope to move people out or around, or even to find better than the present lot, is severely limited.

Better to think of changing the skills, capacities and attitudes of the individual than of removing the individual altogether. People *can* change if they want to, if they know what is wanted and if they have access to the right sort of help. It does however take time, considerable effort and sometimes a lot of resources – which may be the reason that personal development and learning are something which most voluntary organizations leave to the initiative of the individual.

We also know that individuals need different skills as they move up through organizations – see Box 9.6. Professional competence needs to give way to the ability to handle people, create visions of the possible and connect the apparently unconnected as one gets more senior. These abilities do not come to all of us naturally, but they can at least be fostered by careful experiment and reflection. Learning, it has been said, is 'experience understood in tranquillity'. But all three ingredients are necessary: the experience, the understanding and the tranquillity; and they do not happen by chance.

Box 9.6 The skills of an effective administrator

Over thirty years ago Professor Katz laid down what he saw as the necessary skills of the administrator: *technical skills*, *human skills* and *conceptual skills*. He went on to point out that:

- Technical skills are needed principally at the bottom and sides of an organization; human skills mainly in the middle layers; while conceptual skills are crucially important at the top.
- Technical skills can be taught (often in a classroom situation); human skills can be learned but not really taught; while conceptual skills can be developed only if you already have them in embryo to start with. We make a great mistake if we try to turn human or conceptual skills into technical skills just because those are the ones that are teachable.

Which skills do you need to improve?

From Katz, 'The Skills of an Effective Administrator', *Harvard Business Review*, 1956.

Cultural influences

The different cultures of organizations have their preferences when it comes to choosing the levers for change. Those preferred have already been mentioned in Chapter 6. But they need to be restated here if only to make the point once again that wherever you start in Leavitt's diamond of change you need to move each of the other points as well if the change is to stick. Change needs a multicultural approach, which is one reason why it is so difficult.

Zeus characters instinctively like to switch people around. Apollonians prefer to tinker with the structure, to rearrange the roles. Athenians start by asking what the problem is and redefining the task. Dionysians don't change things, they leave them. Start where you want to start, the message of the diamond is, but don't stop there.

More important, however, than the choice of starting-point is the need for a general culture of movement and growth in the organization. If you want an exciting, developing, changing organization, look for one where the individuals are themselves encouraged to be exciting, developing and changing. What does that mean? It means that:

- Individuals are encouraged to invest in themselves, to develop their talents and skills and even to look for ones they didn't know they had. (One organization gives every individual a 'personal education budget' to be spent on their development/training/education.)
- Individuals are encouraged to take initiatives within the boundaries of their do'nuts, to make mistakes even, provided that they learn from those mistakes. Forgive the sinner while you condemn the sin. (How big a mistake can you make without anyone noticing and stopping you? It's a good question to test the real importance of anyone's job.)
- Individuals are genuinely encouraged to set ever-higher standards for themselves and their groups. (One organization encourages '20/20' thinking: 20 per cent more with 20 per cent less each year. It's remarkable how many groups achieve it, but only by changing the way they do things.)
- What we might be or do is as important in all discussions as what we are or have been. (One organization reckons that only two out of five new ideas ever work out, so it

gives a party to the originator of any *failed* idea, *pour encourager les autres*.)

In cultural terms, the mini-Zeus needs encouraging, to be given space to stretch and goals to stretch towards. Dionysians need tolerating, for they sometimes carry the seeds of the future with them. Athenians need to put some of their problem-solving energies to work on the problems of the future. And Apollonians need to be reassured that the world is not getting out of control. Create an atmosphere of creativity and the blocks to change diminish. Encourage experimentation, forgive mistakes, set goals rather than rules, reward energy and enthusiasm rather than passive conformity and soon the problem will be to hold change in check.

The way ahead

Voluntary organizations are going to be more important to society and to individuals in the years ahead. Organizations need to see in this challenge the opportunity to create a new way of organizing. The danger must be that, without better models, they remain the organizations that have sometimes failed us in the past. In this combination of danger and opportunity lies the forthcoming crisis for the voluntary world.

Such a bold statement needs some explaining. By raising the status and cost of jobs, society has consistently, over the last forty years, made work more expensive. That is admirable for those with the jobs, who might wish that the progress had been even faster at times, but it does mean that a lot of work gets priced out of existence – it is just too expensive to pay people job-money to get some work done. Few private citizens can today afford to pay to have their windows cleaned by someone else, their children reared by others, their old folks tended by others for a wage. Few cities can afford to pay the sums needed to have their streets swept as often as they need to be, their houses maintained or their misfortunates cared for. Work is expensive, and its products are very pricey.

In some areas machines will take over. Streets and windows may be cleaned better and more cheaply by machines than by people. Technology has replaced the servant in the home and the assistant in the store. More of that is still to come, in factories, banks, offices and stores. 'Hi-tech', however, in the words of the United States author John Naisbitt (*Megatrends*, Warner Books, 1982), produces a countervailing need for 'hi-touch'. Humanity cannot live by technology alone; indeed, the more technology the more of the human touch we need. The caring, helping and supporting needs of society are set to grow as fast as, if not faster than, technology.

To take but two obvious examples:

- Technology in one shape or another keeps more people alive for longer, but it doesn't give them things to do, friends to be with or point to their lives. Only other human beings can do that.
- Technology and the pressure of economics replace people with machines and call it improved productivity. So it is, but it doesn't do much to make the replaced people more productive, to feel still useful, relevant and mattering. Only other human beings can do that.

No state or private citizen can afford to meet the growing 'hi-touch' needs with people in paid jobs. It would be too expensive. At best they can staff some sort of infrastructure (and it is an urgent priority to decide what that should be) and some sort of emergency or worst-case service. It will never be enough for all. Voluntary work, therefore, has probably got an ever-expanding future in the 'hi-touch' world. Maybe that is good. Maybe it were better that those who help, care and support do so in the gift economy and not the job economy, working from their hearts and not their pockets.

Maybe it is good, too, for the individuals (more of whom will find that a job's lease hath all too short a date) that their skills and qualifications age even more rapidly, and that youth increasingly has a premium, or that their services fit more conveniently into a firm's arrangements when they are part-time not full-time. After all, in 1986 for the first time in over 100 years the proportion of adults of working age in full-time jobs fell below 50 per cent (excluding those shut up in prison, hospital, school or college). The full-time job is now a minority pursuit for the average adult aged between 18 and 65.

For such as these, the part-time voluntary job is not a substitute for 'the real thing' but it is, or can be, an extra dimension of life, one for which they had no time before. When all men and many women worked all day and all week in one job they became what E. M. Forster called cardboard people, with but one dimension to their lives. Some still do that out of choice, in the rat-race, some out of necessity in the slums of the service trades. But for many there is now the chance of a *portfolio* of work, some paid, some partly paid, some given for free. It makes for rounded people, with more than one outlet for their energies and creativity, more than one group of colleagues, more than one set of workplace politics. It means that when one part fails or goes badly, the whole need not be contaminated.

So there is the opportunity: more outlets for voluntary work; more people with time to do it; more chance of more portfolio people; more 'hi-touch' to set against 'hi-tech'.

The danger lies in the shamrock. In its pursuit of efficiency and managerial ease it is tempting for the voluntary organization to staff its *core* with paid full-time professionals, its contractual fringe with other paid individuals or organizations and its flexible labour force with the volunteers. In other words, it may take the refugees from our flexible labour force and put them in another, condemning them to marginality everywhere – not a very satisfying portfolio.

It could be different. The heart of the core will probably always have to be paid full-time professionals, for only they can provide the necessary continuity and assurance of standards. But the core could be very small (as it already is in the best-regulated businesses), the contractual fringe much larger. Now the contractual fringe, made up of the self-employed and the small co-operative or self-managed group, *could* be the volunteers, increasingly well trained and well qualified, giving of themselves professionally for part of their time. The 'pay' which they would receive, in this version of the psychological contract, would be the training and experience that would allow them to feel, and to be, professional.

Could the bigger voluntary organizations become the new colleges of society, providing new skills, new horizons and new lives for its citizens, many of whom feel de-skilled by their earlier experience of life? Should voluntary organizations recognize that they exist at least as much for their workers as for their clients and turn that to positive advantage? Might they not then discover that organizations can enable people as well as use them? Might they not learn to run themselves more like an association than a factory, a partnership of like-minded people rather than a hierarchy of human resources?

This book has attempted to show that this *is* possible; that it is not a dream which flies at the waking day; that the jigsaw of organization is unusual in that the same bits and pieces *can* be put together to make a different picture; that you can write a book about organizations without using the word 'management'.

Appendix

Questionnaire on the Cultures of Organizations

This questionnaire was prepared to help people to work out their own preferred culture and that of the organization they work in.

Use it to help you to relate the discussion of cultures in Chapter 6 to your own situation or use it, in an organization, to compare the different perceptions people have of how it works.

To complete the questionnaire proceed as follows:

- Consider the organization you work for, the whole of it. What sets of values, what beliefs, what forms of behaviour could be said to be typical of it? Look at the four statements under each of the nine headings in the questionnaire. Under each heading rank the four statements in order of 'best fit' to the organization as you see it (i.e. put '1' against the statement that best represents the organization, '2' against the next best and so on). Put the figures in the column headed 'Organization'.
- When you have done this for the organization, then go through the whole process again, this time for yourself, in the column headed 'Self', reflecting your own preferences and beliefs. Try not to look at your rankings under 'Organization' while you do this, so that your second ranking is truly independent.*

* The questionnaire is adapted from one originally developed by Dr Roger Harrison of Development Research Associates.

When you have ranked all the statements under each of the two columns add up the scores for all the statements that are marked (a) under each heading, then the scores for all the statements listed (b), and so on (e.g. a total score of 9 for all the (b) statements would mean that you had ranked the (b) statement '1' in each of the nine headings).

You should now be able to complete the following table.

	All (a) statements	All (b) statements	All (c) statements	All (d) statements	Total
The organization					90
Yourself					90

As in most questionnaires, you will want to qualify many of your answers with the remark 'It all depends . . .' You will find it hard in some instances to find any great difference in your own mind between some of the statements. Don't let this deter you. The questionnaire results will not be precisely accurate, but they should provide useful indications. You will find that the best way to proceed when trying to rank each set of statements is to trust your first, almost intuitive reactions. Don't linger over them too long.

When you have completed the questionnaire and added up the totals, turn to page 167 for an explanation of the scores.

Self		Organization
1	*A good boss*	
(a)	is strong, decisive and firm but fair. He is protective, generous and indulgent to loyal	
____	subordinates.	____
(b)	is impersonal and correct, avoiding the exercise of his authority for his own advantage. He demands from subordinates only that which is required by	
____	the formal system.	____

(c)   is egalitarian and influenceable
            in matters concerning the task.
            He uses his authority to obtain
            the resources needed to get on
____   with the job.   ____

(d)   is concerned and responsive to
            the personal needs and values of
            others. He uses his position to
            provide satisfying and growth-
            stimulating work opportunities
____   for subordinates.   ____

Self   Organization

2   *A good subordinate*

(a)   is hard-working, loyal to the
            interests of his superior,
____   resourceful and trustworthy.   ____

(b)   is responsible and reliable,
            meeting the duties and
            responsibilities of his high job
            and avoiding actions which
            surprise or embarrass his
____   superior.   ____

(c)   is self-motivated to contribute
            his best to the task and is open
            with his ideas and suggestions.
            He is nevertheless willing to give
            the lead to others when they
            show greater expertise or
____   ability.   ____

(d)   is vitally interested in the
            development of his own
            potentialities and is open to
            learning and receiving help. He
            also respects the needs and
            values of others and is willing to
            give help and contribute to their
____   development.   ____

Self		Organization
3	*A good member of the organization gives first priority to*	
(a)	the personal demands of the boss. _____	_____
(b)	the duties, responsibilities and requirements of his own role, and the customary standards of personal behaviour. _____	_____
(c)	the requirements of the task for skill, ability, energy and material resources. _____	_____
(d)	the personal needs of the individuals involved. _____	_____

Self		Organization
4	*People who do well in the organization*	
(a)	are politically aware, like taking risks and operating on their own. _____	_____
(b)	are conscientious and responsible, with a strong sense of loyalty to the organization. _____	_____
(c)	are technically competent and effective, with a strong commitment to getting the job done. _____	_____
(d)	are effective and competent in personal relationships, with a strong commitment to the growth and development of individual talents. _____	_____

Self		Organization
5	*The organization treats the individual*	
(a)	as a trusted agent whose time and energy are at the disposal of those who run the organization. _____	_____

(b)   as though his or her time and
             energy were available through a
             contract, having rights and
_____   responsibilities on both sides.   _____
(c)   as a co-worker who has
             committed his or her skills and
_____   abilities to the common cause.   _____
(d)   as an interesting and talented
_____   person in his or her own right.   _____

Self   Organization
6   *People are controlled and influenced
             by*
(a)   the personal exercise of rewards,
_____   punishments or charisma.   _____
(b)   impersonal exercise of economic
             and political power to enforce
             procedures and standards of
_____   performance.   _____
(c)   communication and discussion
             of task requirements leading to
             appropriate action motivated by
             personal commitment to goal
_____   achievement.   _____
(d)   intrinsic interest and enjoyment
             in the activities to be done;
             and/or concern and caring for
             the needs of the other people
_____   involved.   _____

Self   Organization
7   *It is legitimate for one person to
             control another's activities*
(a)   if he or she has more power and
_____   influence in the organization.   _____
(b)   if his or her role prescribes that
             he or she is responsible for
_____   directing the other.   _____

(c)   if he or she has more knowledge
——   relevant to the task at hand.   ——
(d)   if he or she is accepted by those
——   he or she controls.   ——

Self   Organization
8   *The basis of task assignment is*
(a)   the personal needs and
       judgement of those who run
——   the place.   ——
(b)   the formal divisions of functions
——   and responsibility in the system.   ——
(c)   the resource and expertise
       requirements of the job to be
——   done.   ——
(d)   the personal wishes and needs
       for learning and growth of the
       individual organization
——   members.   ——

Self   Organization
9   *Competition*
(a)   is for personal power and
——   advantages.   ——
(b)   is for high-status position in the
——   formal system.   ——
(c)   is for excellence of contribution
——   to the task.   ——
(d)   is for attention to one's own
——   personal needs.   ——

Interpretation of questionnaire scores

The (a) statements represent the Zeus club culture; the (b) statements represent the Apollo role culture; the (c) statements represent the Athenian task culture; and the (d) statements represent the Dionysian existential culture. The *lower* the total score for any set of statements the *more prevalent*

that culture is in your organization or in you. A score of 9
for the (a) statements (the lowest possible total) would mean
a totally pure Zeus culture. You are unlikely to have any
totals as low as that.

A table that reads, for example:

	(a)	(b)	(c)	(d)	Total
The organization	14	12	27	37	90
Yourself	29	24	16	21	90

would mean that your organization was a mix of Apollo
and Zeus, while you prefer to be Athena backed up by
Dionysus.

Further Reading

There is a multitude of books on and about organizations and management. Only some of them are worth reading. The most relevant ones have mostly been mentioned in the text, and the best are listed here for easy reference.

Adair, J., *Effective Leadership* (Gower, 1983). A self-development manual by the inventor of action-centred leadership; practical and sensible.

Bishop, J., and Hoggett, P., *Organizing around Enthusiasms: Mutual Aid in Leisure* (Comedia, 1986). A delightful description of some unusual collectives, with pertinent analysis.

Child, J., *Organization: A Guide to Problems and Practice* (Harper & Row, 1984). A good but dry overview of the research and theory on organizations by one of Britain's leading authorities.

Drucker, P., *Management* (Pan, 1977). Any book by Peter Drucker is full of insight; this is the big one.

Handy, C., *Understanding Organizations*, 3rd edn (Penguin, 1985). The text on which this book is based; it contains more extensive chapters on all the topics, along with more complete references.

Handy, C., *The Future of Work* (Blackwell, 1984). An analysis of the changing shape of work and organizations in Britain.

Hunt, J., *Managing People at Work* (Pan, 1978, 1986). A well-written, common-sensical overview of many of the topics covered in this book.

Kanter, R. M., *The Change Masters* (Allen & Unwin, 1983). A modern classic; an analysis of corporate entrepreneurs in the United States.

Landry, C., *et al.*, *What a Way to Run a Railroad* (Comedia, 1985). A radical, and stimulating, look at voluntary organizations and the failings of conventional management theories.

Olsen, M., *The Rise and Decline of Nations* (Yale University Press, 1982). A distinguished economist's analysis of change in nation-states; difficult but good.

Peters, T. J., and Waterman, R.A., *In Search of Excellence* (Harper & Row, 1984). The best-selling pop classic on management methods in the USA's best businesses; there is a lot of sense behind the glitz.

Index